Kosmos Knowledge Ecosystems Inc.

D-801, Dheeraj Hill View Tower,

Siddharth Nagar, Borivali (E)

Mumbai – 400 066

Email: eswarier@gmail.com

First Edition – April 2000

Table of Contents

Chapter 3

Chapter 4

Chapter 5

List of Tables

List of Figures

Examples

Preface

Databases can contain vast quantities of data describing decisions, performance and operations. In many cases the database contains critical information concerning past business performance which could be used to predict the future. Often the sheer volume of the data can make the extraction of this business information impossible by manual methods. Data mining is a set of techniques, which allows an organization benefit from tapping the vast resources available with them.

Data Mining (also known as Knowledge Discovery) technology helps businesses discover hidden data patterns and provides predictive information, which can be applied to benefit the business. The basic approach is to access a database of historical data and to identify relationships that have a bearing on a specific issue, and then extrapolate from these relationships to predict future performance or behavior. The human analyst plays an important role in that only they can decide whether a pattern, rule or function is interesting, relevant and useful to an enterprise.

Over the years, many different approaches have been taken to try to extract useful information, or knowledge from the hundreds of gigabytes of information generated by an organization On-line Transaction Processing (OLTP) Systems. Analyzing data can provide further knowledge about a business by going beyond the data explicitly stored to derive knowledge about the business. This is where Data Mining or Knowledge Discovery in Databases (KDD) has obvious benefits for any enterprise.

There has been a dramatic surge in the level of interest in data mining, with business users wanting to take advantage of the technology for competitive edge. The growing interest in data mining has also resulted in the introduction of a myriad of commercial products, with similar terminologies but distinct functionalities and approaches.

Data mining is the computational process of discovering patterns in large data sets with the objective of extracting information and transforming it into an understandable structure for further use. Data mining involves data and database management, pre-processing techniques, model and inference considerations alongwith post-processing of uncovered structures, data visualization, and online updation. Data Mining and Knowledge Discovery in Databases are terms that are generally used interchangeably. The other terms referring to data mining are data or information harvesting, archeology, functional dependency analysis, knowledge extraction and data pattern analysis. Data Mining is used to identify potential knowledge from seemingly plain data sets.

This book provides a solid foundation over which the pillars of advanced mining techniques can be built on. The book commences with an introduction to the basic concepts and terminologies related to data mining. The detailed architecture of data mine, the challenges in handling erroneous data, data mining process as well as the data mining tools are also presented subsequently.

Sudhir Warier

This page is intentionally blank

Acknowledgements

This is to acknowledge the contributions of all the authors of works that have been referred to in this book. In addition I also acknowledge the valuable insights gained from crawling the web, more specifically the websites of application developers. The structure and the presentation style is unique and based on my kndowledge and experiences in the field of Data Warehousing and Data Mining.

This page is intentionally blank

Dedicated to my family

Wife – Priya Sudhir Warier

Son – Neil Sudhir Warier

Mother – Rathy Madhavan

Father – Late C.V. Madhava Warier

This page is intentionally blank

Nomenclature

2D	Two Dimensional
3D	Three Dimensional
CART	Classification and Regression Trees
CHAID	Chi Square Automatic Interaction Detection
CRISP-DM	Cross-Industry Standard Process For Data Mining
DBMS	Database Management Systems
DSS	Decision Support System
EIS	Executive Information System
EQ	Emotional Quotient
Gb	Gigabyte
I/O	Input/Output
IBM	International Business Machines
KDD	Knowledge Discovery In Databases
LHS	Left Hand Side
MPP	Massively Parallel Processing
OLAP	Online Analytical Processing
OLAP	On-Line Analytical Processing
OLTP	On-Line Transaction Processing
OODBMS	Object-Oriented Database Management Systems
POS	Point-Of-Sale
RDBMS	Relational Database Management Systems
RHS	Right Hand Side
SME	Subject Matter Expert
SQL	Structured Query Language

Chapter Objectives

The objectives of this chapter are:

- *To present an introduction to the world of Data Mining*
- *To introduce the terms, technologies and concepts associated with Data Mining*
- *To differentiate between data mining, knowledge discovery in data bases, artificial intelligence, machine learning, decision support systems and other similar sounding techniques*
- *To highlight the importance of analytical processing in the current knowledge industries*

Chapter 1

INTRODUCTION TO DATA MINING

1.1 Need & Progression

The past two decades has seen a dramatic increase in the amount of data as well as information being processed electronically. This accumulation of data has taken place at a fiery rate. The amount of information generated globally doubles every 20 months with the size and number of databases ever increasing. The increase in use of electronic data gathering devices such as point-of-sale (POS) or remote sensing devices has contributed to this explosion of available data. Data storage has become less costly and cumbersome with the developments in computing technologies and the falling prices. In fact computing power, which was once the prerogative of large multinational corporations, has now become accessible to the common man. The introduction of new machine learning techniques for knowledge representation are highly process intensive and has led to the development of multi-core processing technologies. In short the need for processing large volumes of data has significantly contributed to the development of computer processors and storage devices.

There has been a dramatic surge in the level of interest in data mining, with business users wanting to take advantage of the technology for competitive edge. The growing interest in data mining has also resulted in the introduction of a myriad of commercial products, with similar terminologies but distinct functionalities and approaches. The IT managers charged with the task of selecting a decision support system (DSS) often face a challenge in responding to the needs of the business users because the underlying concepts of data mining are far more complex than traditional query and reporting, and to add to the pressure the needs of the business users are usually urgent, requiring decisions that need to be made quickly.

However, while various approaches to data mining seem to offer distinct features and benefits, in fact just a few fundamental techniques form the basis of most data mining systems

Having concentrated so much attention on the accumulation of data the problem was in employing this valuable resource to effective use. It was recognized that information is at the heart of business operations and that decision-makers could make use of the data stored to gain valuable insight into the business. Database Management systems provide access to the underlying data. Traditional On-Line Transaction Processing (OLTP) systems are designed for fast movement of data into a database. However these systems cannot be used for the analysis function. The analysis of data within a database or a warehouse can help unearth previously unknown patterns or knowledge relevant to the business domain. Knowledge Discovery in Databases (KDD) has now become a significant discipline by itself and is an invaluable tool to any business enterprise, irrespective of the industry. The term 'data mining' refers to the extraction of information or knowledge from databases. There are numerous definitions of the term; some of the popular ones are as listed below:

i)   Data Mining, also known as Knowledge Discovery in Databases (KDD), refers to the extraction of implicit, unknown, and useful information and knowledge from data. This includes a number of different approaches, such as clustering, data summarization, learning classification rules, finding dependency networks, analyzing changes, and detecting anomalies (Frawley, Piatetsky-Shapiro, & Matheus, 2001)

ii)   Data mining is the search for relationships and global patterns that exist in large databases but are hidden among the vast amount of data. These relationships embody valuable knowledge about the database, the objects in the database and the real world represented by the database – (Marcel Holshemier & Arno Siebes, 1994)

iii)   Data mining refers to "using a variety of techniques to identify nuggets of information or decision-making knowledge in bodies of data, and extracting these in such a way that they can be put to use for decision support, prediction, forecasting and estimation". The data store is usually very large and the data patterns are not discernable directly. – (Data Mining Toolkit)

Basically data mining is concerned with the analysis of data and the use of software techniques for finding patterns and regularities in sets of data. This is achieved by identifying the underlying rules and features in the data. The Data Mining software extracts patterns not previously discernable or in other words relationships that they have not been noticed previously.

Data mining analysis tends to work from the data up and the best techniques are those developed with an orientation towards large volumes of data, making use of as much of the collected data as possible to arrive at reliable conclusions and decisions. The analysis process initiates with a block of data and employs appropriate methodologies to develop an optimal representation of the data in tune with the knowledge to be extracted. The underlying logic can subsequently be extrapolated to larger data volumes with similar underlying structures. This process can be compared to a physical gold mine where tones of ore have to be sifted in order to extract small amounts of lode containing gold.

The following figure 1.1 summarizes the primary stages and the key processes involved in mining and knowledge discovery in data (Usama Fayyad, Shapiro and Smyth, 1996):

Figure 1.1 - Data Mining Process

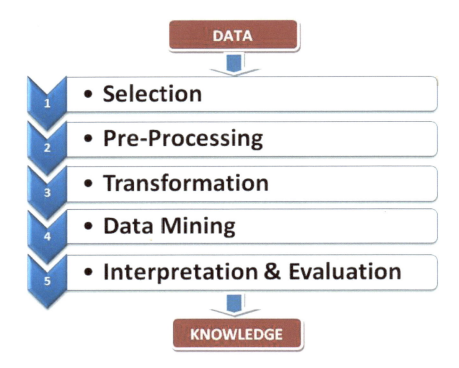

The extraction of knowledge from the raw data is done over five phases as depicted in figure 1.1 and outlined in the section below:

i)   **Selection**

This stage deals with the selection or segmentation of available data according to some fundamental criterion. An example could be "Individuals who own a car". This type of segmentation facilitates determination of subsets within the data.

ii)   **Preprocessing**

This is the data cleansing stage where information that is deemed unnecessary is removed. This is done to prevent the slowing down queries. An example of such data could be the gender of a patient admitted for child delivery. The final data is reconfigured to ensure a consistent of format since the sources of data may be numerous. An example is that the Gender field may contain an alphabet 'M' or 'F' or numeric values '0' and '1' for males and females respectively.

iii)   Transformation

The process of transformation involves the addition of overlays like demography in order to make the data useable and suitable for navigation.

iv)   Data Mining

Data mining is the computational process of discovering patterns in large data sets with the objective of extracting information and transforming it into an understandable structure for further use. Data mining involves data and database management, pre-processing techniques, model and inference considerations alongwith post-processing of uncovered structures, data visualization, and online updation. The term is usually generalized to any refer to computer decision support system artificial intelligence, machine learning, and business intelligence (Wikipedia, 2008).

v)   Interpretation & Evaluation

The patterns identified by the system are interpreted, resulting in knowledge, which can subsequently employed to support human decision-making e.g. prediction and classification tasks, database content summarization or explaining observed phenomena.

1.2   Evolution

Data mining research has drawn on a number of other inter-related disciplines including inductive learning, machine learning and statistical analysis.

i)   Inductive learning

Induction is the inference of information from data and inductive learning is the model building process where the environment (database) is subjected to pattern analysis. Similar objects are grouped in classes and rules formulated whereby it is possible to predict the class of hidden objects. This process of classification results in classes with a unique prototype of values and results in the generation of the class description. It is important to note environment is dynamic in nature and hence an adaptive model should be employed. Generally it is only possible to use a small number of properties to characterize objects, so abstractions are made in the objects that satisfy the same subset of properties and are mapped to the same internal depiction. Inductive learning involves assimilating knowledge from observations related to the environment and is based on two primary strategies:

a) **Supervised Learning**

This method involves learning through the use of examples wherein a model is constructed by defining classes and supplying examples of each class. The system has to find a description or the common properties in the examples related to each class. Once the description has been formulated the description and the class form a classification rule that can be used to predict the class of previously undiscovered objects. Discriminant analysis, a powerful statistical analysis technique, is an example of the above technique.

b) **Unsupervised Learning**

This method of learning involves observation and discovery. The data mining system is supplied with objects but no classes are defined so it has to observe the examples and recognize patterns (i.e. class description) by itself. In case of unsupervised learning a class description would be discovered for each environment.

Induction is therefore the extraction of patterns. The quality of the model produced by inductive learning methods is excellent and can be used to predict the outcome of future situations. This implies that the model can be used for prediction for known as well as unknown states. The challenge lies in the fact that most environments have different states and it is not always possible to verify a model by checking it for all possible situations.

Given a set of examples the system can construct multiple models of differing complexities. This implies that a few models would be simpler in comparison with the rest. These models tends be correct if the developer adheres to Ockham's razor. This principle states that if there are multiple explanations for a particular phenomenon it makes sense to choose the simplest because it is more likely to capture the nature of the phenomenon (Wikipedia, 2008).

(ii) **Statistics**

The field of statistics provides solid theoretical foundations, but the results from statistics can be overwhelming and difficult to interpret. Statistical analysis mandates expert guidance as to where and how to analyze the data. Data mining facilities the seamless assimilation of a subject matter expert's (SME) domain knowledge with advanced analysis techniques and is therefore highly potent. Statistical analysis packages such as SAS and SPSS have been used by analysts to detect and explain unusual patterns using statistical models such as linear models. It is therefore very important to understand that Data mining is not a replacement for statistical analysis but helps in directed analyses based on discovered patterns. For example statistical induction is similar to the average rate of failure of machines.

(iii) **Machine Learning**

Machine learning involves the automation of the learning process and is similar to the construction of rules based on observations of environmental states and transition. Machine learning refers to a wide turf that includes learning from examples, reinforcement learning and learning with an instructor. A learning algorithm takes the data set and its accompanying information as input and returns a concept indicative of learning output. This type of learning involves parsing through prior examples, their outcomes and employing the learning's to provide generalizations about new cases.

Generally a machine learning system does not use single observations of its environment but an entire finite set containing examples representing machine readable observations appropriately coded. The training set is finite hence not all concepts can be learned exactly.

1.3   Knowledge Discovery in Databases

Knowledge Extraction is the creation of knowledge from structured (relational databases, XML) and unstructured (document, text and images) sources. The resulting knowledge needs to be in a machine-readable and machine-interpretable format and must represent knowledge in a manner that facilitates inferencing. Machine learning is a branch of artificial intelligence (AI), which deals with the study and development of systems capable of learning from underlying data. An example of this learning is the mailing systems that are configured to distinguish spam emails from an individual's inbox. The differences between the two are summarized below:

i) KDD is concerned with uncovering knowledge, while ML results in performance improvement of software threads. The specific tasks and subtasks within a neural network is the part of ML, but not of KDD. However the to extract knowledge from neural networks are relevant to KDD.

ii) KDD is concerned knowledge extraction from large corporate databases and warehouses, while ML generally explores smaller data sets. Hence performance and efficiency of the systems is more important for KDD.

iii) ML is a broader field that includes not only learning from examples, but also reinforcement learning and learning with the use of instructor's.

iv) KDD is that part of ML which is concerned with finding understandable knowledge in large databases or warehouses. KDD necessitates the integration of machine-learning techniques onto database systems with the following set of requirements :

    a) More efficient learning algorithms because real world databases are large, noisy and with different levels of normalization. The database is usually designed for purposes different from mining and hence the properties or attributes responsible for the simplification of learning tasks may not be available. Databases are usually dirty due to errored data. Data mining algorithms work around such phenomena while machine learning deals with text book perfect data.

b) More expressive representations for both data, e.g. tuples in relational databases, which represent instances of a problem domain, knowledge and the semantic information contained in the relational schemata (Frawley, Piatetsky-Shapiro, & Matheus, 2001)

The practical implementation of a KDD system involves the following three interconnected phases:

1. Translation of standard database information into a form suitable for use by learning facilities

2. Using machine learning techniques to produce a knowledge base from databases

3. Interpreting the assimilated knowledge to help find solutions to user problems and/or reduce data spaces

1.4   Data Mining Processes

The data mining process must be reliable and repeatable by individuals (domain uses) with little knowledge or no data mining background. A cross-industry standard process for data mining (CRISP-DM) was published with contributions from over 300 organizations (Zentut). There are two types of statistical analysis:

(i)   Confirmatory Analysis

In confirmatory analysis a single hypothesis or multiple hypotheses is formulated and is accepted or rejected based on the findings of the statistical analysis. , one has a hypothesis and either confirms or refutes it. However, the bottleneck for confirmatory analysis is the shortage of hypotheses on the part of the analyst.

(ii)   Exploratory Analysis

In exploratory analysis one finds suitable hypotheses to confirm or refute. Here the system takes the initiative in data analysis, not the user.

The concept of "initiative" also applies to multidimensional spaces. In a simple OLAP access system, the user may have to think of a hypothesis and generate a graph. But in OLAP data mining, the system thinks of the questions by itself. Data mining refers to the automated process of data analysis in which the system takes the initiative to generate patterns by itself.

From a process-oriented view, there are three classes of data mining activity as illustrated in the figure 1.2 below:

(i) Discovery

Discovery is the process of parsing a database to find hidden patterns without a predetermined idea or hypothesis about what the patterns may be. The program takes the initiative in finding what the interesting patterns are, without the user thinking of the relevant questions first. In large databases, there are many patterns that a user could never practically think of the right questions to ask. The key issue here is the richness of the patterns that can be expressed and discovered and the quality of the information delivered -- determining the power and usefulness of the discovery technique.

(ii) Predictive modeling

In predictive modeling patterns discovered from the database are used to predict the future. Predictive modeling helps a user to submit records with some unknown field values, and the system will guess the unknown values based on previous patterns discovered from the database. While discovery uncovers data patterns, these patterns are employed to guess values for new data items in predictive modeling.

(iii) Forensic Analysis

Forensic analysis is the process of applying the extracted patterns to find anomalous or unusual data elements. To discover the unusual, first the normal data is determined, and then those items that deviate from the usual within a given threshold are identified. It is to be noted that discovery helps to find "usual knowledge," but forensic analysis deals with searches for specific unusual or uncommon knowledge.

Figure 1.2 - Data Mining - Process Oriented View

Each of these processes can be further classified. There are several types of pattern discovery mechanisms such as 'If/Then' rules and associations. While the rules discussed above have an 'If/Then' nature, association rules refer to items groupings (e.g., when someone buys one product at a store, they may buy another product at the same time -- a process usually called market basket analysis). The power of a discovery system is measured by the types and generality of the patterns it can find and express in a suitable language (Parsaye, 1996).

1.5 Users and Applications

It is necessary to distinguish the data mining processes discussed above from the data mining activities in which the processes may be performed, and the users who perform them. The three different classes of users usually perform data mining activities in any organization can be classified as below:

(i) Executives

Executives need top-level insights and spend far less time with computers than the other groups -- their attention span is usually less than 30 minutes. They may want information beyond what is available in their executive information system (EIS). End users and analysts usually assist executives

(ii)   Analysts

Analysts interpret data and do occasional computing but are not programmers. They may be business analysts, statisticians, business consultants and database or warehouse developers. These analysts are usually aware of statistics techniques and are familiar with SQL.

(iii)   End users

End users are familiar with basic office suite packages and applications but do not have any programming background. Examples of end users are sales personnel, market research consultants, scientists, engineers, physicians among others. It may be noted that Line Managers often assume the role of both an executive as well as an end user.

These users usually perform the following set of data mining activities within the corporate environment:

i)   Episodic Data Mining

In Episodic mining, data is analyzed from one specific episode such as a specific direct marketing campaign. The resulting data set would be used for further understanding or for prediction on new sales and promotional marketing campaigns. Episodic Mining is generally employed by analysts.

ii)   Strategic Mining

In Strategic mining the larger sets of corporate data are analyzed with the intention of gaining an overall understanding of specific measures such as profitability. Hence, a strategic mining exercise may look to answer questions such as: "where do our profits come from?" or "how do our customer segments and product usage patterns relate to each other?"

iii)   Continuous Data Mining

In continuous mining the emphasis is on understanding how the world has changed within a given time period and try to gain an understanding of the factors that influence change. For instance the following questions may be considered "How have sales patterns changed this month?" or "What were the changing sources of customer attrition last quarter?" Continuous mining is an on-going activity and usually takes place once strategic mining has been performed to provide a first understanding of the issues.

Continuous and strategic mining are often directed towards executives and line managers. It may be noted that diverse types of mining are supported by different technology types.

1.6   Data Mining Models

Data Mining is used to unearth data patterns of interest to a specific class of users. These patterns and trends can be collected and defined as a data mining model. Generally there are two types of models or modes of operation that may be used to unearth information of interest to the user:

(i) Verification Model

The verification model takes a hypothesis from the user and tests the validity of it against the collected data. The emphasis is on the user responsible for the hypothesis formulation and execution of queries with a view of confirming or negating the hypothesis.

Example - 1

In a marketing division for example with a limited budget for a mailing campaign to launch a new product it is important to identify the section of the population most likely to buy the new product. The user formulates a hypothesis to identify potential customers and their shared characteristics. The Historical data about specific customers, their purchase preferences and demographic information can subsequently be queried to reveal comparable purchases. These characteristics can be used as inputs to a promotional or mailing campaign. The entire operation can be refined by `drill down' queries to identify the data set required to hypothesis verification.

Disadvantages

The problem with this model is the fact that no new information is created in the retrieval process but rather the queries will always return records to verify or negate the hypothesis. The search process in this case is iterative in that the output is reviewed and a new set of questions or hypothesis is formulated to refine the search. The whole process repeated again. In the process the user discovers facts about the data using a variety of techniques such as queries, multidimensional analysis and visualization to guide the exploration of the data being inspected (Frawley, Piatetsky-Shapiro, & Matheus, 2001).

(ii) Discovery Model

The discovery model differs in its emphasis in that it is the system automatically discovering important information within the data set. The data is sifted to uncover frequently occurring trends, patterns and data generalizations without user intervention or guidance. The KDD and data mining tools aspire to divulge a large number of facts about the data in a relatively short time span.

Example - 2

An example of such a model is a bank database that is mined to discover the many groups of customers to target for a promotional sales campaign. The data set is parsed with no specific hypothesis in mind with a view to group the customers according to the common characteristics uncovered.

1.7   Data Mining Challenges

Data mining systems rely on databases to supply the raw data for input. This leads to problems due to the fact that databases are usually very large, tend to be updated dynamically, may be incomplete and contain noise or irrelevant information. Other problems arise as a result of the adequacy and relevance of the information stored and is listed below:

i) Limited Information

A database is often designed for purposes different from data mining and sometimes the properties or attributes that would simplify the learning task are not present nor can they be requested from the real world. Inconclusive data causes problems because if some attributes essential to knowledge about the application domain are not present in the data it may be impossible to discover significant knowledge about a given domain. For example one cannot diagnose malaria from a patient database if that database does not contain the patient's red blood cell count.

ii) Noise & Missing Values

Databases are usually contaminated by errors so it cannot be assumed that the data they contain is entirely correct. Attributes, which rely on subjective or measurement judgments, can give rise to errors such that some examples may even be mis-classified. Error in either the values of attributes or class information is known as noise. Obviously where possible it is desirable to eliminate noise from the classification information as this affects the overall accuracy of the generated rules. Missing data can be handles in a variety of methods by the discovery systems. These include:

a) Ignore missing values

b) Delete entire records corresponding to missing values

c) Extrapolate missing values from known values

d) Handle missing data as special values to be included additionally in the attribute domain

e) Average missing values using Bayesian techniques.

Noisy data is a characteristic of data sets and typically fit a regular Gaussian statistical distribution. Wrong values are treated as typo or data entry errors and are handled by the statistical techniques employed.

iii) Uncertainty

Uncertainty refers to error severities and the degree of noise in the data. Data precision is an important consideration for a knowledge discovery system.

iv) Consistency

Databases tend to be large and dynamic with their contents subjected to regular addition, deletion or modification. This presents a challenge as data mining system requires current and consistent data and information. The challenge lies in ensuring the updation of rules are up-to-date and ensuring consistency with the most current information. The learning system is generally time-sensitive and is affected by data values that vary over time.

v) Context

The issue of relevance or irrelevances of the fields in the database to the current focus of discovery are fundamental to establish a connection between items of interest.

1.8 Applications

Data mining has many and varied fields of application some of which are listed below.

(i) Retail/Marketing

Following are some of the areas that could benefit from the deployment of a Data Mining solution:

- Identify buying patterns from customers
- Discover associations within customer demographic characteristics
- Predict typical responses to promotional campaigns
- Market Basket Analysis

(ii) Banking

Data Mining has extensive scope of usage within the Banking Industry and Financial Services. Following are some of the key usage areas:

- Detect credit card usage patterns including fraudulent use
- Customer loyalty analysis
- Identifying most valuable customers
- Predict customers likely to drop off
- Identify card spending patterns
- Co relational analysis

(iii) **Insurance and Health Care**

The list presented below represents the common application of Data Mining within the Insurance and Health Care segments:

- Claims Processing & Analysis
- Predict potential customers
- Segregating high risk customers and their buying patterns
- Identify behaviors of fraudulent customers

(iv) **Transportation**

Depending upon the scope and the requirements within an organization, data mining solutions could be deployed extensively for analysis with comprehensive benefits, as mentioned below:

- Determine the distribution schedules among outlets
- Analyze loading patterns

(v) **Medicine**

The list mentioned below presents a small insight into the potential usage of OLAP solutions in the fields of medicine and the medical industry as a whole:

- Characterize patient behavior to predict office visits.
- Identify successful medical therapies for different illnesses

1.9 Summary

Data Mining and Knowledge Discovery in Databases are terms that are generally used interchangeably. The other terms referring to data mining are data or information harvesting, archeology, functional dependency analysis, knowledge extraction and data pattern analysis. Data Mining is used to identify potential knowledge from seemingly plain data sets. The Data mining process involves a number of processes and mandates the amalgamation of human expertise alongwith analytical technologies and tools. Machine learning is a branch of artificial intelligence (AI), which deals with the study and development of systems capable of learning from underlying data. Knowledge Extraction is the creation of knowledge from structured and unstructured sources. The resulting knowledge needs to be in a machine-readable and machine-interpretable format and must represent knowledge in a manner that facilitates inferencing.

1.10 Exercise Questions

1. What is meant by Data Mining? Briefly discuss its significance in today's industry?
2. Explain the phases involved in the process of Data Mining.
3. Discuss the various fields that impact or contribute to the development of Data Mining Solutions.
4. Explain in detail the various Data Mining processes.
5. Discuss the various Data Mining Models.

This page is intentionally blank

Chapter Objectives

The objectives of this chapter are:

- *To broadly present the various techniques employed in the field of Data Mining*
- *Data mining methods may be classified by the function they perform or according to their application class usage. The primary mining techniques are introduced in this chapter:*
    - *Classification*
    - *Associations*
    - *Sequential/Temporal Patterns*
    - *Clustering/Segmentation*
- *Understand the primary techniques for Data Mining & Analysis including:*
    - *Cluster Analysis*
    - *Induction*
    - *Decision Trees*
    - *Rule Induction*
    - *Neural Networks*
- *Describe the concept, functions as well as challenges of On-line Analytical Processing*

Chapter 2

DATA MINING TECHNIQUES

2.1 Introduction

Over the years, many different approaches have been employed to extract useful information, or knowledge from the hundreds of gigabytes of information generated by an organization On-line Transaction Processing (OLTP) Systems. Traditionally the primary source of access and analysis were simple report generators and query tools. The advent of data warehousing improved the scope and breadth of the reporting tools that has resulted in a vast improvement in their capability and potential impact. A query is the simplest method for accessing a database to request information. Query and reporting tools enable users to formulate queries without having to interact with and create code with the SQL programming language, and also offer formatting and presentation templates to display the results. Some even offer the ability to move the results into spreadsheet packages to derive graphical representation of the results, or have graphic capabilities included in them directly. In order to use a standard query tool for information discovery, the user must first develop a hypothesis based on observations or intuition, and create questions (queries) to test the validity of the hypothesis. This is known as the verification-driven approach. While these tools provide easy to use interfaces and rich formatting and graphical presentation, the quality of the analysis is only as good as the observation powers and intuition of the analyst. Further, simple query tools are limited in the scope of the complexity of queries that can be generated and the complex joins and other database manipulations that can be performed.

Organizations basically deploy two kinds of systems, which are those that run the business and create data and those that report on the business and access data.

OLTP systems are the ones that run the business e.g. Order entry systems, reservations systems etc. E.F. Codd in 1993 introduced the concept of Online Analytical Processing (OLAP) in a white paper that established twelve rules and defined its difference from simple database query and reporting tools and more sophisticated analytic methods. OLAP functions as the access point to obtain information in the data warehouse and is reserved for sophisticated multi-dimensional analysis.

2.2 Analytical Processing

Analytical Processing functions have come primarily to mean multidimensional analysis of the data warehouse and have been often confused with query and reporting tools, statistical analysis and data mining. OLAP differs from the simpler query tools in their ability to manipulate data cubes in real time and to perform a number of analytical functions upon them. This kind of complex OLAP functionality or multidimensional data analysis requires robust data computational and data navigation capabilities. As pointed out before, Multidimensional Analysis allows users to formulate much broader questions than traditional query and reporting systems would allow. Users can enter the data warehouse from any single dimension and begin the analysis, and then navigate to other dimensions to continue the analysis. The OLAP process is an interactive process and the resulting reports used by users are continually modified as the analysis progresses. These require a computational layer of software that transforms data in the warehouse into information. The computational layer, including summarized data, can easily generate four to five times the amount of data as the original facts stored in the data warehouse.

Statistical analysis is a complex process that attempts to reduce a large amount of data to a simple relationship, which is often stated as a mathematical formula. More sophisticated statistical functions include regression, factor analysis, correlation and cluster analysis. Data interpretation tools support advanced analysis of data. Examples include business statistics and optimization (linear programming).

Data Interpretation is a broad class of data access provided by predefined reports. These models are important for answering "what-if types" of questions. They are used to generate models that project customer sales or customer behavior on relationships and historic trends. In all of these tools, the differentiator in the quality of the analysis is the analyst's brain. It is the analyst who decides to look at the relationships between products and stores over a particular time period, or over a demographic spread, etc. Therefore, while OLAP has proven to be a very useful tool in data access and analysis, there is still a need for more automated approaches, which are less resource intensive.

Example - 3

If an organization has four hundred products that are sold through six store chains in sixty states over a twelve-month period, the number of facts to sift through are 400 x 6 x 60 x 12 = 1.7 million facts. The example presented here has only four dimensions to be considered. It is not unusual to see situations with six, seven or more dimensions, each of which can have tens of possibilities. The permutations are staggering. Somewhere in that mammoth number there may be a particular view of the facts, according to a certain set of dimensions that can give an organization the competitive advantage over its rivals.

2.3   Data Mining Techniques

Data mining methods may be classified by the function they perform or according to their application class usage. The primary mining techniques are as listed:

2.3.1 Classification

Data mining tools help in inferring models from datasets within a database. This activity necessitates the definition of one or more classes by the user. The database includes attributes denoting tuple (ordered list of elements) classes which are referred to as predicted attributes. The remaining attributes are referred to as predicting attributes. A class is defined as a combination of values for the predicted attributes. The rules that predict a class from the predicting attributes are learned by the system. This requires that the user defines conditions for each class, and the mining system constructs descriptions for the classes subsequently. The system should be provided with a case or tuple with certain known attribute values to be able to predict the class for specific. Subsequent to class definition, the system should infer rules that govern the classification and locate the description of each class. The descriptions should only refer to the predicting attributes of the training set so that the positive examples satisfy the description and none of the negative examples do so. A rule is deemed to be correct if its description covers all the positive examples and none of the negative examples of a class. A rule is generally presented as, if the left hand side (LHS) then the right hand side (RHS), so that in all instances where LHS is true then RHS is also true, is very probable. The categories of rules are:

i) Exact rule - permits no exceptions so each object of LHS must be an element of RHS

ii) Strong rule - allows some exceptions, but the exceptions have a given limit

iii) Probabilistic rule - relates the conditional probability P (RHS|LHS) to the probability P (RHS)

Other types of rules are classification rules where LHS is a sufficient condition to classify objects as belonging to the concept referred to in the RHS.

2.3.2 Associations

Association function is an operation on a given collection of items and a set of records, each of which contain some number of items from the given collection, which return affinities or patterns that exist among the collection of items.

Example - 4

These patterns can be expressed by rules such as "64% of all the records that contain items A, S and W and also contain items B and C." The specific percentage of occurrences is referred to as the confidence factor of the rule. Also, in this rule, A, S and W are said to be on an opposite side of the rule to B and C. Associations can involve any number of items on either side of the rule.

A typical application that can be built using an association function is Market Basket Analysis. An example of this application could be the execution of an association function on the daily point-of-sale transaction logs of a retailer. The log may contain sales information along with transaction identifiers and product identifiers. The set of products identifiers listed under similar transaction identifiers constitutes a record. The result of this association would be a list of product affinities.

Example - 5
By invoking an association function, the market basket analysis application can determine affinities such as "20% of the time that a specific brand of toothpaste is sold, customers also buys a toothbrush and mouthwash."

Example - 6
Another example of the use of associations is the analysis of the claim forms submitted by patients of a motor insurance company. Every claim form contains the work done on a vehicle following a claim incident. By defining a list of all the works that fall under the purview of the insurance contract and the records that form the part of each unique claim the application can find, using the association function, relationships among certain incident type and the work done.

2.3.3 Sequential/Temporal Patterns
Sequential/temporal pattern functions analyze a collection of records over a period of time to identify trends. The customer identity can be used to uncover patterns from the collection of purchase transactions executed over a period of time. These are typical of direct sales application for an online merchant wherein all transactions are tied to a customer login and profile. Such collection of records

can be analyzed with a sequential pattern to detect frequently occurring patterns of products bought over time. A sequential pattern operator could also be used to discover for example the set of purchases that frequently precedes the purchase of a book.

Sequential pattern mining functions are quite powerful and can be used to detect the set of customers associated with some frequent buying patterns. Use of these functions for example on a set of insurance claims can lead to the identification of frequently occurring sequences of medical procedures applied to patients, that can further help identify good medical practices as well as to potentially detect some medical insurance frauds.

2.3.4 Clustering/Segmentation

Clustering and segmentation are the processes of creating a partition so that all the members of each set of the partition are similar according to a specified metric. A cluster is a set of objects grouped together owing to their similarities or nearness. Objects are often decomposed into an exhaustive and/or mutually exclusive set of clusters. Clustering is a very powerful technique that can translate some intuitive measure of similarity into a quantitative measure. In case of unsupervised learning a system has to discover its own classes i.e. the system clusters the data in the database. The system has to parse data in order to discover subsets of related objects in the training set. Subsequently the descriptions that explain each of these subsets have to be defined. There are a number of approaches for forming clusters. One approach is to form rules that dictate membership in the same group based on the level of similarity between members. An alternative approach would be to build set functions that measure some property of partitions as functions of some parameter of the partition.

Example 7 - Market Basket Analysis

Segmentation techniques can be employed in Market Basket Analysis on Point-of-Sales (POS) transactions where they separate a set of untagged input records into reasonable groups according to product revenue by market. The individual market baskets are segmented based on the number and type of products. The total revenues and number of baskets is collated segment wise. The following types of analysis are generally available,

    i)   Revenue by segment

    ii)   Baskets by segment

    iii) Average revenue by segment

2.4 Analytics

Data mining involves semi-automatic or automatic analysis of large quantities of data to extract previously unknown interesting patterns such as groups of data records (cluster analysis), unusual records (anomaly detection) and dependencies (association rule mining) using appropriate techniques as listed below:

2.4.1 Cluster Analysis

In an unsupervised learning environment the system has to discover its own classes and one way in which it does this is to cluster the data in the database. The first step is to discover subsets of related objects and then find descriptions e.g. Des_1, Des_2, Des_3 etc. which describe each of these subsets. Clustering and segmentation basically partition the database so that each partition or group is similar according to some specified criterion. Clustering based similarity is a technique that is employed across multiple disciplines. If a measure of similarity is available there are a number of techniques for forming clusters. Group Membership can be based on the level of similarity between members. The membership rules can be defined using the created groups. Another approach is to build a set of functions that measure some property of partitions, groups or subsets as functions of some parameter within the partition. This approach helps in achieving optimal partitioning. Clustering based on a set of optimized functions is used in data analysis – for example determining tariffs for customers based in a number of parameters in order to ensure optimal tariff segmentation, by insurance companies.

Clustering/segmentation in databases are the processes of separating a data set into components that reflect a consistent behavior patterns. The established patterns are subsequently employed to "deconstruct" data into understandable subsets and also they provide sub-groups of a population for further analysis or action that is important when dealing with very large databases.

2.4.2 Induction

A database is a store of information. However the information, which can be inferred from it, is of prime importance. There are two main inference techniques available. They are:

i) **Deduction**

Deduction is a technique to infer information that is a logical consequence of the information in the database. An example could be a join operator applied to two relational tables to infer the name of the employee, their employee code and their reporting managers.

ii) **Induction**

Induction is a technique used to infer information generalized from the database. In continuation from the above example one could infer that every employee (of a specified class) within an organization is assigned an employee code and a reporting manager. This constitutes a higher-level information or knowledge about an object or relationships between objects.

2.4.3 Decision Trees

Decision trees are simple representation of knowledge used to classify examples onto a finite number of classes. The nodes are labeled with attribute names and the edges are labeled with possible values for this attribute. The leaves are labeled with different classes. Objects are classified by following a path down the tree, taking the edges, corresponding to the values of its attributes.

The following is an example of objects that describe the categories of automobiles available for purchase. The objects include information on the type of automobile as well as fuel used. Based on these parameters recommendations has been specified. Classification is in this case the construction of a tree structure, illustrated in the following figure 2.2, which can be used to order all the objects correctly.

Figure 2.1 – Decision Trees

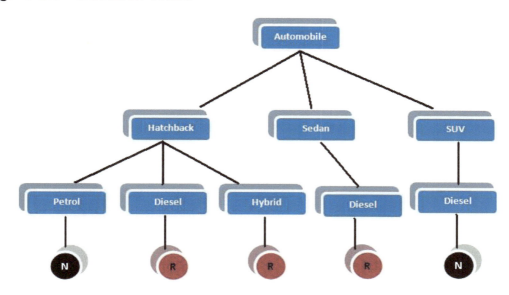

2.4.4 Rule Induction

A data mining system has to infer a model from the database that defines classes such that the database contains one or more attributes that denote the class of a tuple. These represent the predicted attributes while the remaining attributes are the predicting attributes. When the classes are defined the system should be able to infer the rules that govern classification. In other words the system should be able to locate the description of each class. Production rules have been widely used to represent knowledge in expert systems and they have the advantage of being easily interpreted by human experts because of their modularity i.e. a single rule can be understood in isolation and does not require reference to other rules.

2.4.5 Neural Networks

Neural networks represent an approach to computing that involves developing mathematical structures with the ability to learn. The methods are the result of academic investigations to model learning systems similar to the human nervous system. Neural networks exhibit remarkable abilities to derive meaning from complicated or imprecise data and can be used to extract patterns and detect trends that are too complex to be noticed by either humans or computer techniques. A trained neural network can be thought of as a "subject matter expert (SME)" in the category of information being analyzed. This SME can subsequently be employed to provide projections for new situations of interest and provide answers to "what if" questions. Neural networks can be used for providing solution to a range of real world business problems and have already been successfully applied in many industries. Neural networks are apt at identifying patterns or isolating trends in data. This makes them suitable for prediction or forecasting needs including:

i)   Sales Forecasting
ii)   Industrial Process Control
iii) Customer Research
iv)   Data Validation
v)   Risk Management
vi)   Target Marketing

Neural networks use a set of processing elements (or nodes) analogous to neurons in the brain. These processing elements are interconnected in a network that can then identify patterns in data subsequent to an initial exposure. These networks are capable of learning from experience in a fashion similar to human beings. This capability separates a neural network from traditional computing systems that sequentially execute a set of instructions with a computer program. The figure 2.2 approximates the structure of a neural network.

Figure 2.2 – Neural Networks

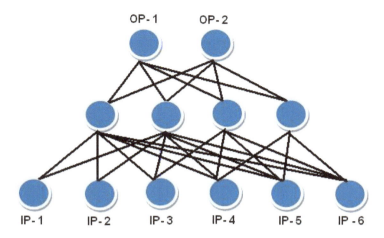

The bottom layer represents the input layer and the inputs are labeled as IP1 through IP5. The middle layer is referred to the hidden layer and consists of a variable number of nodes. This layer performs the bulk of the network function. The output layer is represented by two nodes, OP1 and OP2 representing values that are determined from the inputs. An example could be the sales prediction for a super market based on historical data, price advantages as well as seasonal demands. Each node in the hidden layer is fully meshed with the inputs and the learning is based on the information garnered collectively from all the inputs. Neural networks have been used successfully for the classification function. However the resulting network is viewed as a black box and no explanation of the results is given. This lack of explanation inhibits confidence, acceptance and application of results. Neural networks also require a large amount of time that increases exponentially with the volume of data handled.

2.5   On-line Analytical Processing

A major challenge for information processing systems is to arrive at an optimal process to handle large databases with data of increasingly complex data, without compromising on provides business enterprises an opportunity to deploy specialized servers optimized for handling data management. Generally organizations tend to employ relational database management systems

(RDBMS) for the complete spectrum of database applications. It is however apparent that there are major categories of database applications which are not suitably serviced by relational database systems. Oracle, for example, has built a totally new Media Server for handling multimedia applications. Sybase uses an object-oriented DBMS (OODBMS) designed to handle complex data such as images and audio. Another category of applications is that of on-line analytical processing (OLAP). OLAP was a term coined by E F Codd (1993) and was defined by him as: the dynamic synthesis, analysis and consolidation of large volumes of multidimensional data. The OLAP system requirements are as follows:

i)   Multidimensional Conceptual View
ii)   Consistent Reporting Performance
iii)   Client/Server Architecture
iv)   Generic Dimensionality
v)   Dynamic Sparse Matrix Handling
vi)   Multi-User Support
vii)   Unrestricted Cross Dimensional Operations
viii) Intuitive Data Manipulation
ix)   Flexible Reporting
x)   Unlimited Dimensions & Aggregation Levels
xi)   Transparency
xii)   Accessibility

An alternative definition of OLAP has been coined by Nigel Pendse who defines OLAP as, Fast Analysis of Shared Multidimensional Information. This implies the following:

i)   Quick response times – Instantaneous response to queries
ii) Intuitive analytical functions
iii) Provision for business logic and statistical analysis relevant to the user application.
iv) Concurrent multi user support

v) Multidimensional conceptual with support for multiple hierarchies

A multidimensional database must be able to present complex business calculations in a simplified manner. The data must be referenced and mathematically defined. In a relational system there is no relation between line items, which makes it very difficult to express business mathematics. Intuitive navigation facility should be provided in order to locate data that requires mining hierarchies. The system should be capable of responding instantaneously to users queries Dimensional databases are not suited to storing data types like lists. Relational systems have superior security features, backup and replication mechanisms. These features cannot be directly replicated in dimensional systems. The advantages of a dimensional system are the freedom offered to users to explore the data and receive the reports in a variety of formats.

Example - 8

An OLAP database may comprise of sales data that has been aggregated by region, product type, and sales channel. A typical OLAP query might access a multi-gigabyte/multi-year sales database in order to find all product sales in each region for each product type. After reviewing the results, an analyst might further refine the query to find sales volume for each sales channel within region/product classifications. As a last step the analyst might want to perform year-to-year or quarter-to-quarter comparisons for each sales channel. This whole process must be carried out on-line with rapid response time so that the analysis process is undisturbed. OLAP queries can be characterized as on-line transactions which:

i) Access very large amounts of data, e.g. several years of sales data
ii) Analyze the relationships between many types of business elements e.g. sales, products, regions, and channels
iii) Involve aggregated data e.g. sales volumes, budgeted dollars and dollars spent
iv) Compare aggregated data over hierarchical time periods e.g. monthly, quarterly and yearly

v) Present data in different perspectives e.g. sales by region vs. sales by channels by product within each region

vi) Involve complex calculations between data elements e.g. expected profit as calculated as a function of sales revenue for each type of sales channel in a particular region

vii) Are able to respond quickly to user requests so that users can pursue an analytical thought process without being stymied by the system

OLAP applications are quite different from On-line Transaction Processing (OLTP) applications that consist of a large number of relatively simple transactions. The transactions usually retrieve and update a small number of records that are contained in several distinct tables. The relationships between the tables are generally simple.

Example - 9

A typical customer order entry OLTP transaction might retrieve all of the data relating to a specific customer and then insert a new order for the customer. Information is selected from the customer, customer order, and detail line tables. Each row in each table contains a customer identification number that is used to relate the rows from the different tables. The relationships between the records are simple and only a few records are actually retrieved or updated by a single transaction. The difference between OLAP and OLTP can been summarized as follows:

i) OLTP servers handle mission-critical production data accessed through simple queries; while OLAP servers handle management-critical data accessed through an iterative analytical investigation. Both OLAP and OLTP have specialized requirements and therefore require special optimized servers for the two types of processing.

ii) OLAP database servers use multidimensional structures to store data and relationships between data. Multidimensional structures can be best visualized as cubes of data, and cubes within cubes of data. Each side of the cube is considered a dimension. Each dimension represents a different category such as product type, region, sales channel, and time. Each cell within the multidimensional structure contains aggregated data relating elements along each of the dimensions.

For example, a single cell may contain the total sales for a given product in a region for a specific sales channel in a single month. Multidimensional databases are a compact and easy to understand vehicle for visualizing and manipulating data elements that have many inter relationships. OLAP database servers support common analytical operations including: consolidation, drill-down, and "slicing and dicing".

iii)   *Consolidation*

Consolidation involves the aggregation of data such as simple roll-ups or complex expressions involving inter-related data. For example, sales offices can be rolled-up to districts and districts rolled-up to regions. OLAP data servers can also go in the reverse direction and automatically display detail data that comprises consolidated data. This is called drill-downs. Consolidation and drill-down are an inherent property of OLAP servers.

iv)   *Slicing and Dicing*

Slicing and dicing refers to the ability to view the database from different viewpoints. One slice of the sales database might show all sales of product type within regions. Another slice might show all sales by sales channel within each product type. Slicing and dicing is often performed along a time axis in order to analyze trends and find patterns.

v)   OLAP servers have the means for storing multidimensional data in a compressed form. This is accomplished by dynamically selecting physical storage arrangements and compression techniques that maximize space utilization. Dense data (i.e., data exists for a high percentage of dimension cells) are stored separately from sparse data (i.e., a significant percentage of cells are empty). For example, a given sales channel may only sell a few products, so the cells that relate sales channels to products will be mostly empty and therefore sparse. By optimizing space utilization, OLAP servers can minimize physical storage requirements, thus making it possible to analyze exceptionally large amounts of data. It also makes it possible to load more data into computer memory that helps to significantly improve performance by minimizing physical disk I/O.

In conclusion OLAP servers logically organize data in multiple dimensions, which allows users to quickly, and easily analyze complex data relationships. The database itself is physically organized in such a way that related data could be rapidly retrieved across multiple dimensions. OLAP servers are very efficient when storing and processing multidimensional data. RDBMS have been developed and optimized to handle OLTP applications. Relational database designs concentrate on reliability and transaction processing speed, instead of decision support need.

Data visualization makes it possible for the analyst to gain deep and intuitive understanding of the data and complements standard data mining tools. Data mining allows the analyst to focus on certain patterns and trends and perform an in-depth analysis of the underlying data using visualization. The volume of data in a database can overwhelm the visualization process. The use of data mining tolls can help overcome this obstacle and facilitate exploration.

2.6 Challenges

The typical users requiring access to analytical tools are ignorant of the commercial business applications and provides little attention or credence to the adaptation of high performance computers to business environments. The business database programmers, who are well versed in database management and applications are unfortunately are unaware of parallel processing applications. The challenge is for the database software developers to create easy-to-use tools and form strategic relationships with hardware manufacturers and consulting firms in order to come out with user friendly applications.

Parallel processors can easily assign small, independent transactions to different processors. With more processors, more transactions can be executed without reducing the throughput. This same concept applies to executing multiple independent SQL statements. A set of SQL statements can be broken up and allocated to different processors to increase speed. Multiple data streams allow several operations to proceed simultaneously. A customer table, for example, can be spread across multiple disks, and independent threads can search each subset of the customer data. As data is partitioned into multiple subsets performance is increased. I/O subsystems then just feed data from the disks to the appropriate threads or streams. An essential part of designing a database for parallel processing is the partitioning scheme. Because large databases are indexed, independent indexes must also be partitioned to maximize performance. There are five partitioning methods used to accomplish this:

i) Hashing – Data assignment to disks based on a hash key
ii) Round-robin Partitioning – Sequential assignment of row to partitions
iii) Allocating rows to nodes based on ranges of values
iv) Schema Partitioning - Ties tables to specific partitions
v) User-defined roles.

Oracle was the first to market parallel database packages with their flagship product, ORACLE7 RDBMS. Ease of use is an important factor in the success of any commercial application. The complexities of data layout may be kept transparent from the users. Users who wish to add disks or processor nodes can do so without complex data reorganization and application re-partitioning. The Parallel Server technology performs both the parallelization and optimization automatically, eliminating the need to re-educate application developers and end users. It is also easy for user organizations to deploy because it eliminates many traditional implementation burdens.

2.7 Summary

Corporate databases offer unique challenges to individuals and software developers trying to glean information and knowledge from them. A typical corporate data warehouse contains voluminous stores of data. Any process or tool that operates on this data must be able to efficiently deal with large data sets that may be sparse with a few examples to prove or disprove the existence of a relationship. The challenge of extracting useful information from these databases provided new analytical processing challenges and opportunities that are addressed by data mining techniques and tools. Data mining tools use a discovery-driven approach wherein advanced automated technologies and algorithms are applied to detect trends, patterns, and correlations hidden in the data. Data Mining allows the use of pattern recognition technologies to sort through the warehouse, data marts and databases to uncover and report on patterns and anomalies. This provides decision makers with clearly defined areas to target for further analysis. The data mining tools have a few similarities to the artificial intelligence concepts. However these tools are designed to work with large data sets as well as warehouses. The growth of parallel processing and allied technologies have provided a fresh impetus to the data mining arena leading to the development and deployment of powerful visual analytical packages. The deployment of these tools help business enterprises respond to customer needs and design product and services facilitated by quick and effective decision making capabilities.

2.8 Exercise Questions

1. Briefly discuss the various Data Mining functions.
2. List down the various techniques used in the field of Data Mining along with their salient features.
3. Discuss the relevance of Neural Networks in the field of Data Mining.

4. What is meant by OLAP? Discuss the differences between OLAP & OLTP systems.

5. Discuss the important parameters to be taken into account for developing an OLAP system.

Chapter Objectives

The objectives of this chapter are:

- *To understand new capabilities and business opportunities provided by Online Analytical Processing and Data Mining which are integral parts of any decision support process*
- *To reinforce the learning of some of the mining techniques introduced in the previous chapter including:*
  - *Artificial Neural Networks*
  - *Genetic Algorithms*
  - *Decision trees*
  - *Nearest Neighbour Method*
  - *Rule induction*
  - *Data visualization*
- *To present the Data Mining Architecture*
- *Introduce the foundations for multi-dimensional and influence-based objects.*
- *Understand the concept of an influence domain which is the logical equivalent of a cube in a multi-dimensional space.*
- *Describe the following commonly employed data mining classes:*
  - *Associations*
  - *Sequential patterns*
  - *Classifiers*
  - *Clustering*
- *Understand the three components that are essential for understanding a model:*
  - *Representation*
  - *Interaction*
  - *Integration*

Chapter 3

DATA MINING ARCHITECTURE

3.1 Introduction

OLAP and data mining are integral parts of any decision support process. Traditionally most OLAP systems have focused on providing access to multi-dimensional data, while data mining systems have dealt with "influence analysis" of data along a single dimension. OLAP and data mining should not be considered as separate pillars of the decision support framework, but should be fully merged, as they are inherently related activities that reinforce each other. A uniform framework is required for dealing with relational databases. The concept of OLAP Data Mining is illustrated in the table 3.1:

Table 3.1 – Data Mining – OLAP Usage

Mechanism	Data Space	Aggregation Space
Access/Look-up	SQL Engine	OLAP/ROLAP Systems
Analysis/Discovery Engine	Data Mining	OLAP Data Mining

OLAP users require answers to questions like "What were sales by state by month". However, access alone is not sufficient, since it only provides brief glimpses and snap-shots of the information buried within the data. There exists a need to mine the data along multiple dimensions to find the vast range patterns that exist in the OLAP space, e.g. how are profits influenced by "specific cities on a monthly basis" (Parsaye, 1995).

3.2 Data Mining Dimensions

Decision support applications must consider data mining within multiple dimensions while OLAP systems need to focus on discovery as much as on access. OLAP and data mining must work together within the framework of this theory to avoid getting incorrect results. Unlike operational systems in which design errors can cause poor system performance and hence come to light relatively quickly, mistakes caused by the shortcomings of decision support applications may not be noticed for a long time while significantly impacting the functioning of the associated systems within an organization.

Data mining, ***the extraction of hidden predictive information from large databases***, has a high potential to help modern day service oriented organizations by predicting future trends and behaviors thereby allowing them to make proactive, knowledge-driven decisions. The automated, perspective analysis offered by data mining move beyond the analyses of past events provided by retrospective tools. Data mining provides answers to business questions that traditionally were too time-consuming to resolve. Data mining tools scour databases for hidden patterns, finding predictive information that experts may miss because it lies outside their expectations.

Data mining techniques can be implemented rapidly on existing software and hardware platforms to enhance the value of existing resources, and can be integrated with new products and systems as they are brought on-line. When implemented on high performance client-server or parallel processing computers, data mining tools can analyze massive databases while providing answers to questions such as, "Which customers are most likely to respond to the next promotional mailing, and why?"

Data mining derives its name from the similarities between searching for valuable business information in a large database - for example, finding linked products within volumes of data. This process requires either sifting through an immense amount of material, or intelligently probing it to find exactly where the value resides. Given databases of sufficient size and quality, data mining technology can generate new business opportunities by providing the following capabilities:

i. **Automatic Prediction of Trends and Behaviors**

Data mining automates the process of finding predictive information in large databases. Questions that traditionally required extensive hands-on analysis can now be answered directly from the data very quickly. A typical example of a predictive problem is targeted marketing. Data mining uses data of past promotional mailings to identify the targets most likely to respond to future mailers. Other predictive problems include forecasting bankruptcy and other forms of default, and identifying segments of a population likely to respond similarly to given events.

ii. **Automatic Discovery of Previously Unknown Patterns**

Data mining tools sift through databases and identify previously hidden patterns. An example of pattern discovery is the analysis of retail sales data to identify seemingly unrelated products that are often purchased together. Other pattern discovery problems include detecting fraudulent credit card transactions and identifying anomalous data that could represent data entry keying errors. Data mining techniques can yield the benefits of automation when implemented on existing software and hardware platforms. They can be implemented on new systems, as existing platforms are upgraded and new products developed. When data mining tools are implemented on high performance parallel processing systems, they can analyze massive databases in minutes. Faster processing means that users can automatically experiment with more models to understand complex data. High speed makes it practical for users to analyze huge quantities of data. Larger databases, in turn, yield improved predictions.

iii. **Higher Dimensionality**

In hands-on analyses, analysts must often limit the number of variables they examine because of time constraints. This increases the probability of discarding variables that carries information about unknown patterns being discarded because they are seemingly unimportant. High performance data mining allows users to explore the full dimensionality of a database, without preselecting a subset of variables.

iv. Larger Samples

Larger samples yield lower estimation errors and variance, and allow users to make inferences about small segments of a population. Data mining and Artificial Intelligence are some of the key technologies that have had a major impact across a wide range of industries. In fact parallel processing architectures and data mining had witnessed significant growth in the past decade. The rapid advancements in data capture, transmission and storage, necessitates the implementation of new and innovative ways to mine the vast stores of detail data, employing Massively Parallel Processing [MPP] systems to create new sources of business advantage.

Data mining tools can be used to automate more elements in the process of building risk models for a variety of markets. Data mining can present business managers with the top ten most significant new buying patterns each week, or with patterns of sales calls and marketing promotions that have significant impact within certain market niches. Some of the most commonly used techniques in data mining are:

i. Artificial Neural Networks

These refer to non-linear predictive models that learn through training and resemble biological neural networks in structure

ii. Genetic Algorithms

Optimization techniques that use processes such as genetic combination, mutation, and natural selection in a design based on the concepts of natural evolution

iii. Decision trees

Decision trees are tree-shaped structures that represent sets of decisions. These decisions generate rules for the classification of a dataset. Specific decision tree methods include Classification and Regression Trees (CART) and Chi Square Automatic Interaction Detection (CHAID). CART and CHAID are decision tree techniques used for classification of a dataset. They provide a set of rules that one could apply to a new (unclassified) dataset to predict which records will have a given outcome.

iv. **Nearest Neighbour Method**

The Nearest Neighbour technique classifies each record in a dataset based on a combination of the classes of the k record(s) most similar to it in a historical dataset (where k 1). It is also referred to as the k-nearest neighbor technique.

v. **Rule induction**

Rule induction refers to the extraction of useful if-then rules from data based on statistical significance.

vi. **Data visualization**

The visual interpretation of complex relationships in multidimensional data is referred to as visualization.

Data mining techniques are the result of a long process of research and product development. This evolution began when business data were first stored on computers, continued with improvements in data access, and more recently, generated technologies that allow users to navigate through their data in real time. Data mining takes this evolutionary process beyond retrospective data access and navigation to prospective and proactive information delivery. Data mining is supported by three mature technologies which include:

a. Data collection and storage
b. Multi core processing and parallel processing
c. Data mining algorithms

Commercial databases are growing at unprecedented rates. The accompanying need for improved computational engines can be met in a cost-effective manner with parallel multiprocessor computer technology. Data mining algorithms embody mature, reliable and easy-to-understand tools and techniques that consistently outperform older statistical methods.

3.3 Data Mining Architecture

The OLAP based data mining architecture draws on the structure of Decision Support systems. OLAP mining takes place on the hybrid space formed by data, aggregation and influences. As shown in Figure 3.1, OLAP based mining engines accesses both the data space and the aggregation space via an SQL engine and an OLAP/ROLAP engine.

Figure 3.1 – Data Mining Architecture

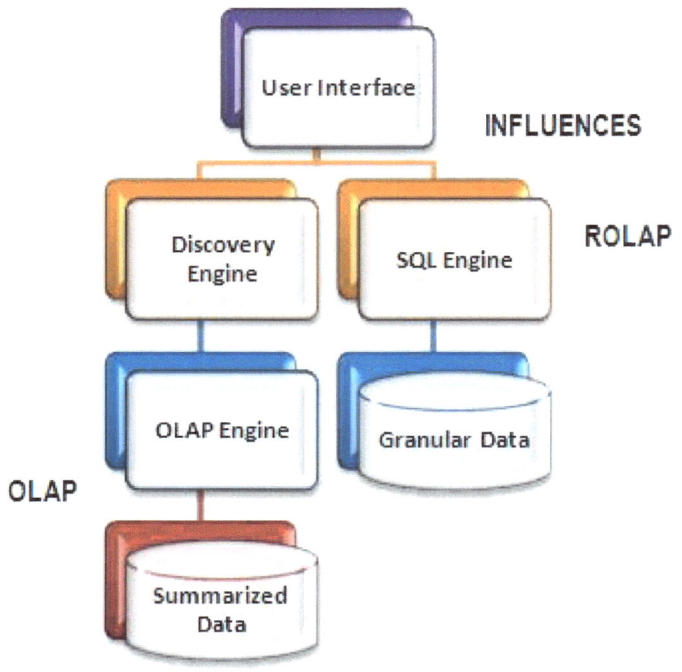

The primary components of an OLAP Data Mining System are as follows:

- A relational database for storing the granular data. However this need not be a data warehouse and could be a data mart or a data mine.
- A multi-dimensional OLAP or ROLAP engine which provides fast access to summary data along multiple dimensions.
- A multi-dimensional discovery engine that performs discovery along multiple dimensions, and merges the results. Such engine accesses both

the granular data via SQL and the multi-dimensional data via the OLAP/ROLAP engine.

The OLAP Discovery Engine provides access to the hybrid space of influences over data and aggregations, merging and combining the results. Without OLAP mining key pieces of information may result in incorrect results, as illustrated by the simple example below. Posing a simple series of logical questions can provide a clear rationale for OLAP applications:

i.   Does granular data have patterns?

ii.   Does summarized data have patterns?

iii.   Does data summarized along different dimensions have different patterns?

iv.   Do summarized patterns relate to each other and to granular patterns?

v.   Should data be mined along both granular and summarized dimensions?

vi.   Should granular and summarized patterns be merged and analyzed?

vii.   Is OLAP based mining necessary to discover these patterns?

The example shown below demonstrates how misleading results can be obtained mining is not properly performed on multiple dimensions. It also brings out the inadequacies of flat files in dealing with multi-dimensional data mining.

Example - 10

The following example uses a simple sales table (Table 3.2) consisting of three products, three stores and profits.

Table 3.2 – Store Details

Product	Product Color	Product Price (INR)	Store	Store Size	Profit (INR)
Shirt	Blue	220	S1	1000	-200
Shirt	Blue	220	S2	5000	-100
Shirt	Blue	220	S3	9000	700
Tie	Green	70	S1	1000	30
Tie	Green	70	S2	5000	-100
Tie	Green	70	S3	9000	-100
Socks	Green	50	S1	1000	20
Socks	Blue	50	S2	5000	-30
Socks	Green	50	S3	9000	-20

The goal of data mining is to find patterns of influence. For instance, how does product color or store size affect profits? To simplify the process we will concentrate on finding out patterns that provide us information about the status of the profits. The table depicted above cannot be subjected to analysis with any one of the well known methods of influence detection such as, decision trees, simple rules, belief networks, neural networks etc. All these methods are designed to determine likelihood and most can trace part of their roots to probability theory. Because they measure likelihood's, they are inadequate for dealing with influences within aggregation space. Based on the standard methods one can conclude that a blue shirt is profitable only in large stores (>9000). However it does not convey the amount of profit and the associated factors influencing it. Likelihood's alone are cannot provide information for effective decision-making. This requires the use of aggregations or looking at likelihood's along multiple dimensions. It is important to note that the even though the top-level rules may appear similar, but in the OLAP space, the likelihood behavior begins to diverge. Let us assume another store with similar products but with slightly different operating margins. A straight comparison of the two tables may not reveal any significant patterns. However if one were to depict another table with the aggregation of the profits across various store sizes, a totally different pattern starts to emerge. The analysis may be somewhat more complicated than it might have looked earlier. A study of the two aggregations may lead to the emergence of other related issues.

The simple statements that may be generated from various views may not mean what the user expects, because they refer to the likelihood of a product being profitable, not the actual values. The likelihood statements typically do not include dimensions. The above example highlights why an OLAP access can also be misleading. A user may, on a cursory examination of data, infer that blue products are profitable, and then stock up on blue items in the stores that they own. Another OLAP user may draw a significantly different conclusion from the tabulated data. Most OLAP users do not have enough time to analyze all of the relevant scenarios and hence may get ambiguous or incorrect conclusions.

The above example illustrates the problems associated with the use of the obvious methods of analysis provided by the conventional flat analysis methods. Likelihood's provide fine-grained information in most of the simple cases but would entail machine assistance to handle more complicated cases. The analysis of complex cases necessitate the usage of an OLAP Data Mining system that mines along multiple dimensions, is aware of the patterns along these dimensions, merges them and interacts with the user in an intelligent manner. Such multi-dimensional data mining provides information such as: "Blue products are profitable overall, but much of the profits come from ties in large stores" and "Green products are profitable too, but mostly in small stores."

This is only possible by combining likelihood computations with aggregations. In fact, whenever data mining takes place, it happens within some "dimension", and data mining along a single axis is merely a rough approximation of multi-dimensional mining. Lack of attention to dimensionality in data mining can result in unexpected results. When dealing with multi-dimensional data, any approach to data mining that preprocesses numeric values to transform them to non-numeric code values (e.g. a flat file) will totally fail in dealing with OLAP patterns.

3.4   Multi-Dimensional Objects

One of the essential factors for the success of relational databases and SQL is the existence of a well-founded mathematical models and language. The figure 3.2 below illustrates the foundations for multi-dimensional and influence-based objects. The basic concept is to manipulate items within a multi-dimensional or influence space, as one manipulates relational elements. Viewing these elements as objects helps produce a robust structural framework for dealing with dimensions and attributes. The basic unit of a multi-dimensional space is a *cube*, just as the basic unit of the relational world is a table. Cubes have attributes, just as relations have columns. The word cube suggests three dimensions, but if not confined to them and can involve multiple dimensions depending upon the tool being employed. (For e.g. Microsoft SQL Server 7.0 supports upto 64 dimensions). The basic components include:

    i.   Classes or base dimensions
    ii.   Attributes
    iii.   Objects or instances (each with a unique identifier)
    iv.   Hierarchies
    v.   Values for attributes
    vi.   Measurements

A base dimension is a class such as: Product, Store, Customer, etc. Each class/dimension may have a set of attributes, for instance the dimension Customer may have the attributes Age, Income, etc.; the dimension Store may have the attributes Size, Chain, etc. and the dimension Product may have the attributes price, color, category, etc.

Each class has objects or elements as instances, for instance the class Customer has an object or element "Neil Warier" or "Rathy Madhavan", and the object Product may have an object instance such as "Niligiri Apples", or "Tata's Salt". Each of the attributes of the object will then have a "value", e.g. Neil Warier may have age 7, while Tata's Salt may be priced at Rs. 7.00.

Hierarchical properties may be present within the classes and attributes. For instance, a class called Brand may be a parent class for a Product. And the attribute manufacturer is inherited by Product from Brand. However it may be noted that one can still perform computations over Brands as though they were classes by themselves. Similarly, stores are grouped together by zones, cities by state, states by regions, etc. The concept of {city, state, region} is a hierarchy.

A "star schema" usually maps directly into the object structure discussed. All that is required is to allow each dimension table to become an object, the attributes of the object then represent the columns in the dimension table, as shown in Figure 3.2.

Figure 3.2 – Star Schema

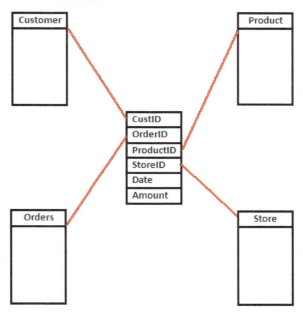

A measurement is a computation over the space formed by the dimensions, for instance Sales, Profits, Margins, etc. Measurements are almost always numeric computations, while the other attributes may be numeric or non-numeric. Each cube represents an aggregate computation over the set of dimensions, for instance sum of sales for all products in all stores, or the sum of sales for all products in just one store. A point in a cube is called a coordinate or an instance, e.g. sales for Oranges in Store at Thakur Village. The value of a measurement is computed based on a cube. For instance, sales by state gives us an array the states, with values for sales. The algebra of cubes provides operations on cubes just as the relational algebra provides operations on tables. A cube may projected i.e. A dimension may be discarded. The projection effectively performs an aggregation over the discarded dimension, e.g. if we have "sales by state by month" and project out month, one just get sales by state. Selection is also easy, e.g. given "sales by state by month" one can select with "where State= Maharashtra or Kerala" to get another cube. However, more interestingly, inter-cube aggregate operations are needed, e.g. One can operate on "sales by state by month" and "expense by state by month" to get "profit by state by month". The main note of caution here has to do with hierarchical relationships, e.g. moving from products to brands.

The OLAP space is a derived space from the relational space that provides more flexible and efficient access to the multi-dimensional data. In a relational space, the concept of aggregation (often involving a table scan) is secondary to indexed access, while the reverse is true in the OLAP representation.

3.5 Influence Domains

An influence domain is the logical equivalent of a cube in a multi-dimensional space. While a cube holds summarized data or aggregations, an influence domain provides information about implications. Like a cube, an influence domain has attributes and values and delivers confidence factors, not just sums of numbers such as sales. For instance it provides information such as the confidence that a product color influences profits. The confidence is usually represented as a number between 0 and 100%.

An influence domain is in effect a function, mapping intervals from the pair consisting of a cube and a measure to a linear measure of confidence. For instance, as in Figures 3.3 and 3.4, given the pair (Coordinate, Measure) where Coordinate is a triple (Kerala, May, Yellow) from the axes (State, Month, Product Color) and the measure Profit, the influence domain gives us a confidence of 75% about the influence of Yellow products in Kerala on measures such as sales or profits. This is different from the representation in cubes.

Figure 3.3 – Representing Influence Domains

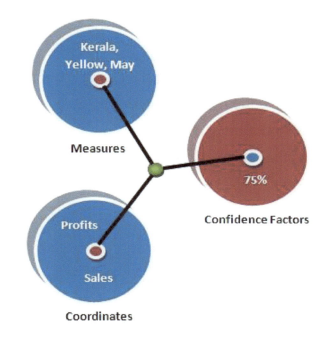

Figure 3.4 – Representing Cubes

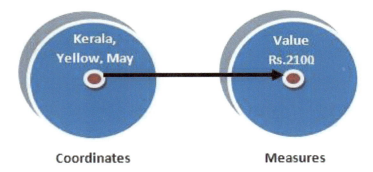

The numeric ranges need to be managed very carefully. For e.g. when dealing with the influence of discount-level on profits. Coding numeric ranges into constants (as many traditional agent systems do) will cause major problems.

Many of the available algorithms for decision trees, belief networks, neural nets, etc. do not work well for multi-dimensional discovery due to three main issues:

i.   These algorithms are derived using theorems from probability and statistics, hence they compute likelihood's, not aggregations

ii.   They process one table at a time and hence tend to miss other dimensions.

iii.   They need to break numeric values into specific ranges; hence missing key patterns along multiple dimensions.

Dealing with influence domains requires a new theory, new data structures and algorithms. Similar to the distinction between OLAP and the relational space, one needs to understand that influence domains are just as different from OLAP and star schemas as they are from relational spaces. The table 3.3 below shows how each computational space needs a distinct approach.

Table 3.3 – Influence Domains

System	Theory/Method	Basic Token	Data Structures
Relational	Relational Algebra	Relations	Third Normal Form
OLAP	OLAP Algebra	Cubes	Star Schemas
Data Mining	Influence Algebra	Influence Domains	Rotational Schemas

It should be clear that star schemas alone are not sufficient for representing influence domains. Star schemas were designed to deal with aggregations, not influence analysis. They work well for OLAP, but not for OLAP Data Mining. To deal with influence domains one needs to extend star schemas. The size of an influence domain is typically much larger than the size of the cube on which the domain is based. Thus, to traverse the influence domain, one needs to interleave OLAP computations with influence analysis. The need for interleaved computations arises due to the fact that one is dealing with a hybrid space in the context of the four spaces of decision support.

These influence computations need to take place on schemas which store more aggregations than a star. The cost of recomputed the aggregations would be very high. At each point during the influence analysis one needs to focus on some dimension table (e.g. Product or Store) within the star, and for each such dimension table one needs to further data than the star typically stores. The focus of the analysis moves clockwise from Customer, to Store to Product, etc. During this clockwise movement one needs to focus on the dimension table with additional aggregated or selected data items. The focus of the analysis seems to be rotating around the star and hence these structures are known as rotational schemas. As illustrated in figure 3.5, a table in a rotational schema has five main parts:

    i.   Focus dimension (e.g. Customer)

    ii.   Measure computed for the focus (e.g. Profit, etc.)

    iii.   Internal attributes (e.g. Customer Age, etc.)

    iv.   External attributes (e.g. favorite product color for that Customer, etc.)

    v.   Non-focused measures (e.g. average number of items per purchase by the Customer).

In the process of OLAP discovery, the focus rotates along the various dimension tables as one traverses the hybrid space to perform influence analysis. This is also reflected in the architecture shown in Figure 3.1, where the OLAP Discovery Engine can interleave calls to the OLAP engine and the SQL engine with influence computations, as the focus rotates around the star from one dimension table to another.

Figure 3.5 – Rotational Schema

Rotational schemas, as illustrated in the figure 3.5 above, is to be used only in Data Mines and nor data warehouses. Rotational schemas are suitable for the influence space, not for the data space. Rotational Schemas also require large-scale data structuring. However, various minor design decisions for the warehouse make the creation of rotational schemas within the Data Mine much more convenient and efficient. A good trade-off involves the use of a slightly modified star schema for the warehouse and rotational schemas for the mine.

The algebra of influence domains provides operations on influence factors just as the cube algebra facilitates OLAP operations. A domain may be projected or a dimension may be discarded. The projection effectively performs a new influence computation without the discarded dimension, e.g. if the influence domain represents "sales by state by month" and project out month, the result would be sales by state domain. The interesting inter-domain operation here is influence stratification by overlap reduction, i.e. determining how influences have hidden interactions and discounting the overlaps which must be done quite carefully. The main note of caution here is that if one is not extremely cautious, one can get incorrect results much more quickly than in other cases.

A natural way of representing this structure is to use the methods or categories and – "DSS-algebras" as a mathematical structure whose elements are the algebras, and whose mappings relate the algebras together. This category will provide a uniform setting for dealing with all the mathematical foundations required for decision support.

3.6   Data Mining Models

Data mining involves extracting hidden information from a database. The underlying process may be complicated; however the user is unaware of the operations being performed on the data. Data Visualization tools help a user to understand the operations being performed within a database along with the underlying structure. Competitive business pressures and a desire to leverage existing information technology investments have led many firms to explore the benefits of data mining technology. This technology is designed to help businesses discover hidden patterns in their data especially those patterns that can help them understand the purchasing behavior of their key customers, detect likely credit card or insurance fraud, predict probable changes in financial markets, etc (Kurt Thearling, Barry Becker, Dennis DeCoste, Bill Mawby, Michel Pilote, and Dan Sommerfield, 1998)

.

Many firms have invested heavily in information technology to help them manage their businesses more effectively and gain a competitive edge. Over the last three decades, increasingly large amounts of critical business data have been stored electronically and this volume is expected to continue to grow considerably in the near future. However, only a handful of companies have realized the benefits of data mining and allied tools and techniques. The information or patterns that are implicit in the data is not easy to discern. For example, a retail store may keep detailed information about the purchases made by each customer every day but still have difficulty pinpointing many subtle buying patterns. Similarly, an insurance firm may keep detailed historical information about claims that have been filed, and still have difficulty isolating some of the likely indicators of fraud.

Advances in the field of Data mining are helping customers leverage their data more effectively and obtain insightful information that can provide them a competitive edge. The data mining software enables customers to discover previously undetected facts present in their business critical data. The data, amounting to terabytes, may reside in flat files, various databases, relational database management systems located on a variety of operating system platforms. The architecture (open architecture support), accuracy and efficiency of the data mining software play an important part in determining its usage.

Organizations from a number of industries including retail, finance, healthcare and insurance routinely maintain enormous amounts of data about the activities and preferences of their customers. Implicit within this data are patterns that reveal the typical behaviors of these consumers, behaviors that can help firms fine-tune their marketing strategies, reduce their risks, and effectively improve their bottom lines. For example, retailers often wish to know what products typically sell together. Knowing that 70 percent of their customers who buy a certain brand of cold drink also buy a certain brand of potato chips can help the retailer determine appropriate promotional displays, optimal use of shelf space, and effective sales strategies. As a result of performing these types of affinity analyses, a retailer might decide not to discount the potato chips whenever the cold drink is on sale, as doing so would needlessly reduce profits.

A somewhat similar requirement is to understand historical buying patterns over a large time interval. For example, one such pattern might be that 64 percent of the people who order a certain type of trouser and belt will order a shirt within a short span of time. The awareness of such crucial information can help online retailers narrow down the scope of a given promotional campaign or perhaps help in designing custom mailers leading to an increase success rate of its promotional campaigns.

Multiple industries, traditional as well as modern service oriented, have similar requirements to detect hidden patterns in the stored data. The stored data can be diverse in nature including those related to oil exploration and drilling, stock markets, consumer specific data among others. The challenge faced by most business enterprises is in detecting patterns in these large complex data sets within a reasonable time frame and at an acceptable cost. This are the areas where technology becomes a major enabler and contributes to the enhancing the value of a business enterprise.

3.6.1 Industrial Applications

The finance and insurance industries have long recognized the benefits of data mining. The growth and the cost effectiveness of the software industry has helped in percolating the benefits of data mining application to previously unchartered industries. These include:

Retail/Marketing

    i.   Identifying customer behavior and buying patterns

    ii.   Customer demographic associations

    iii. Predict response to promotional mailers

Banking

    i.   Detect patterns of fraudulent credit card usage.

    ii.   Predict customer loyalty

    iii. Predict customers likely to switch loyalties

    iv. Determine categorized spending patterns of customers – credit and debit

    v.   Discover hidden correlations between different financial indicators.

    vi. Identify stocks trading rules from historical market data.

Insurance and Health Care

    i.   Claims analysis – Determine common medical procedures

    ii.   Predict new customers

    iii. Identify behavior patterns of high risk customers.

    iv. Identify fraudulent behavior

Transportation

    i.   Determine the distribution schedules among outlets.

    ii.   Analyze bottlenecks and loading patterns.

Medicine

    i.   Characterize patient behavior to predict office visits.

    ii.   Identify successful medical therapies for different illnesses.

3.6.2 Discovery versus Verification

Decision Support Systems (DSS), Executive Information Systems (EIS), and query/report writing tools are used to generate reports about data, usually aggregating it through multiple dimensions. Another use of these tools is to detect trends and patterns in customer data that will help answer fundamental business questions. When used in this mode, a query is created to access the records relevant to the question(s) being formulated. After the data is retrieved, it is examined to detect the existence of patterns or other useful information that can be used to answer the original question(s). This is referred to as the verification mode. A DSS user generates a hypothesis based on the underlying data, issues a query against the data and examines the results of the query in order to accept or reject the hypothesis. The process terminates in case the hypothesis is accepted by the user. In case of rejection the query has to be reformulated and the process iterates until the resulting data either verifies the hypothesis or the user decides that the hypothesis is not relevant to the data being examined.

Example - 11

A sales executive has a limited budget for a new product promotional campaign. In order to optimize the use of this money, the marketing executive wants to identify the set of people that are the most likely to buy the new product and can be targeted within the available budgets. On the basis of these requirements the executive formulates a hypothesis and queries the database with the historical sales and customer demographic data. Appropriate filtering criteria may be specified in order to limit the size of the records retrieved from the database. For example the most likely customers are females in the age group of 22 to 30 years with an annual income of over one lakh rupees. If the result of this query returns a number of customers that match the available budget for mailing promotions, the process ends. However, if either significantly more (or less) customers are found than the number that can be reached with the given budget, a new query limiting (or expanding) the set of customer addresses requested must be issued.

In the above example, the hypotheses used in formulating the queries were quite explicit (age group, gender, annual income) Even when the hypotheses are implicit, the process of finding useful trends or patterns using queries can be described by the above behavior. This concept is explained through the following example.

Example - 12

After a report that presents significantly low sales for a quarter, the business head of a division wants perform a root cause analysis. This necessitates an initial query for the sales figures, by region, for the last quarter. The results of this query would indicate the regions where the sales have been lower than expected. The business head conjures a few hypotheses to explain the low sales in the region. To better understand the nature of the problem, another query is issued that will return sales results for all the cities in the offending region. The result indicates that one city has reported significantly lower sales. This result may be in conformance of the business manager's initial implicit hypothesis (es). Subsequent queries may continue to drill down the data set searching for results by store within the offending city or totally new queries would be fired if the results of the previous queries were contradictory to the implicit hypothesis (es).

Queries, such as those used in the previous two examples, always return records that satisfy the query predicates. Thus, little new information is created in this retrieval process: either the hypothesis is verified or it is negated. The user does the process of information finding by successive iterations upon examining the results of query after query and linking the verified and refined hypotheses. This is the essence of a verification model.

Many times, while performing a query, a request is made to compute functions related to the records being inspected during the query (e.g., count the number of records; find the average of a given field of the records, etc.) All these operations result in additional information being returned together with the query. The use of queries to extract facts from databases is a common practice. There are other tools that, like query generators, are used in a mode that follows the verification model described above. Examples of these other tools are:

i.   Multidimensional analysis tools
ii. Visualization tools

Multidimensional tools make it easier for the user to formulate drill down queries such as described in example 12. Visualization tools facilitate user interaction with the data in search of hidden patterns. The user of a visualization tool takes advantage of the human's visual perception capabilities to discern patterns. The three types of tools discussed above, queries, multidimensional analysis and visualization facilitate user exploration of the underlying data sets.

Data mining uses a different model for the creation of information about data. This model is referred to as the discovery model. This necessitates the development of methodologies that can sift through the data in search of frequently occurring patterns, can detect trends, produce generalizations about the data, etc. These tools must be capable of discovering the required types of information with very little (or no) guidance from the user. A well-designed data-mining tool has an architecture that facilitates the exploration of the data in a manner that yields a large a number of useful facts about the data in the shortest amount of time.

The process of sifting through vast data sets to mine information can be compared to that of diamond mining. Prospectors drill holes in a lode with the expectation of discovering diamonds. The process is however very slow, painstaking and not guaranteed to provide results. Knowledge Discovery on the other hand can be compared to the process of emptying the entire contents of the lode onto an open field, wherein the glittering diamonds can be easily identified and sorted.

In Data Mining, large amounts of data are inspected and facts or information are uncovered. However these facts or information are not easily discernable to users, like the glittering diamonds, and requires the application of business logic by the user.

3.6.3 Technology Enablers

There are a number of data mining methods. One way to classify them is by the function they perform. Another way is to classify them according to the class of applications that they can be used in. The following are the commonly employed data mining classes:

(i)   Associations

An association function is an operation against a set of records, which return affinities that exist among the collection of items. This is true for a given collection of items and a set of records, each of which contain some number of items from the given collection. These affinities can be expressed by rules such as "72% of all the records that contain items A, B and C also contain items D and E." The specific percentage of occurrences is called the **confidence factor** of the rule. It may also be noted that in the above example, A, B and C are said to be on an opposite side to the rule to D and E. Associations can involve any number of items on either side of the rule.

Example - 13

A typical application that can be built using an association function is Market Basket Analysis. A retailer can execute an association operator over the point of sales transaction log which contains the transaction and product identifiers. The log contains a collection of items or product descriptors or SKU's. The set of products identifiers listed under the same transaction identifier constitutes a record. The output of the association function is a list of product affinities. Thus, by invoking an association function, the market basket analysis application can determine affinities such as "40% of the time that a specific brand of trousers is sold, customers also buys shirts.

Example - 14

Another example of the use of associations is in an application that analyzes the claim forms submitted by claimants to a motor insurance company. Every claim form contains a set of a work done on the specified vehicle following an incident. By defining the set of work items that can be claimed and the records corresponding to each claim form, the application can find, using the association function, relationships among works that are often performed together.

(ii)   Sequential patterns

In the example 13 discussed above, the identity of the customer that did the purchase is not generally known. If this information exists, an analysis can be made of the collection of related records of the same structure as above (i.e., consisting of a number of items drawn from a given collection of items). The records are tied to profile of the customer performing repeated purchases. This application is typical of online or direct retailers. In this case the retailer or the catalog merchant has information on the customer as well as their purchases, probably over a fairly large amount of time. In order to detect occurrence patterns that can accurately predict customer behavior, a sequential pattern function can be executed. A sequential pattern operator could also have been used discover the purchases preceding the purchase of a toothpaste.

Example - 15

Another example of the use of this function could be in the discovery of a rule that states that 68% of the time when Stock A increased its value by at most 15% over a 5-day trading period, Stock B also increased its value between 18% and 21% during the same period and the increase in the stocks of A & B were followed by 30% increase in value of Stock C during the subsequent week.

Sequential pattern mining functions are quite powerful and can be used to detect the set of customers associated with some frequent buying patterns. Use of these functions on the set of insurance claims discussed above can lead to the identification of frequently occurring sequences of medical procedures applied to patients. This can help identify good medical practices as well as to potentially detect some medical insurance fraud.

(iii)   Classifiers

Classifiers are functions that examine a set of tagged records and produces descriptions of the characteristics of records for each of the classes. It is assumed that there is a given a set of records, each comprising of a number of attributes, a set of tags (representing classes of records) and an assignment of a tag to each record. The class description generated by a classification operator may be explicit (e.g., a set of rules describing each class) or implicit (e.g., a mathematical function which gives the class to which a record belongs to when this record is given as input to this function). These class descriptions can be used to tag new records by determining which class they fall into. The embodiment of the class descriptions is sometimes called a model. Many classification models have been developed. Typical ones are linear regression models, decision tree models; rules based models and neural network models. Decision tree classifiers are examples of explicit classifiers while neural network classifiers are examples of the implicit type.

Example - 16

An example of the classification function is Credit Card Analysis. In fact the classification function is the most apt for tagging customers for financial service providers.

A credit card issuing company may have records about its customers, each record containing a number of descriptors, or attributes. For those customers for which their credit history is known, the customer record may be tagged with a GOOD, MEDIUM or POOR tag, meaning that the customer has been placed in the corresponding risk category.

A classifier function can examine these tagged records and produce an explicit (or implicit, depending on the model) description of each of the three classes. An explicit model (such as a decision tree model) may be used if the application wishes to determine a description of each class of customers. Such a classifier would produce a description of the set of GOOD customers as those with "annual incomes over INR 7, 50,000, age brackets between 35 and 45 and who resides in "South Mumbai neighborhood".)

An implicit model like Neural Networks can be effectively employed in an image identification application. The neural network classification model would be developed using as input a set of image features, or attributes, together with a tag (VALID, INVALID). The resulting model is a trained neural net, which can be used to determine which class a given image belongs to.

Classification functions have been used extensively in classification applications such as credit risk analysis, portfolio selection, health risk analysis, image and speech recognition, etc.

(iv) **Clustering**

Clustering functions produce explicit or implicit descriptions of the different segments produced. The goal of a cluster function is to produce a reasonable segmentation of the set of input records according to specified criteria. The criteria itself is defined by the clustering tool. Thus, different clustering functions may produce different segmentations of the set of input records.

In contrast to the classification operator whose input is a set of tagged records, the input to a clustering operator is a collection of untagged records. Generally there is no knowledge of the classes at the time of application of a clustering operator.

Examples of applications that can use clustering functions are market segmentation, discovering affinity groups, defect analysis, etc. Many of the mathematical technologies that can be used to build classification functions can also be used to build clustering functions.

Many times it is noted that data mining operators can be used cooperatively. For example, an association operator can be used to identify groups of products that have high propensity to be purchased together or a sequential pattern function can identify groups of customers that are likely to purchase some item after they have purchased others. These groupings can then be used to drive a classification function that produces a generalized description of products (or customers) in this class. If the marketing manager of an appliance manufacturer wants   to sell a new product such as a microwave oven, a sequential pattern data mining operation can be deployed to pinpoint significant classes of customers whose buying patterns lead them to purchase microwave ovens. Utilizing these buying patterns one could use a classification method to characterize those sets of customers whose buying patterns follow the identified ones. These sets of customers are most likely to purchase a microwave in the future and so the marketing campaign is targeted to them.

The above categorization is intended to be quite general. There is an extensive body of technology that exists and continues to evolve that can be used to construct data mining functions such as the four mentioned above. In the past, both Classification and Clustering functions have been widely utilized in various forms in Decision Support Systems. To a lesser extent, some Decision Support Systems have provided limited Association functionality. IBM has developed technologies that allow for the implementation of very powerful association and sequential pattern functions.

3.6.4 Data Mining Repository Framework

Data mining tools discover useful facts buried in the raw data. They complement the use of queries, multidimensional analysis and visualization tools to gain a better understanding about data. A well designed Decision Support system as illustrated in the figure 3.6 should provide facilities to perform queries and data visualization as well as provide for powerful data mining operators. The figure illustrates the architecture of a structured data-mining environment. Much like a regular mining process, which takes raw material as it may exist in a mine and through several steps extracts from the ore valuable metals, data mining comprises three distinct phases or steps as mentioned below:

    i.   Data Preparation

    ii.   Mining Operations

    iii. Presentation

The process of information discovery can be described as iteration over the three phases of this process.

Figure 3.6 – Enterprise Data Mining

Phase – I: Data Preparation

The data preparation phase involves two distinct sub-phases as listed below:
  i.   Data Integration and Data Selection
  ii. Pre-analysis

Data Integration refers to the process of merging data residing in an operational environment having multiple files or databases. Resolving semantic ambiguities, handling missing values in data and cleaning dirty data sets are typical data integration issues. Mining does not require that a Data Warehouse be built. Often, data can be downloaded from the operational files to flat files that contain the data ready for the Data Mining analysis. However in many situations Data Mining can and will be performed directly from a Data Warehouse. Other issues that occur during integration, and are specific to Data Mining, deal with identifying the data required for mining and eliminating bias.

For example, to discover product affinities in market basket analysis one may include information about advertising and shelf placement. Bias in the data can result in the discovery of erroneous information. For this reason bias in data should be detected and removed prior to performing the mining operations. As a result of the Data Integration step, data is placed in a Data Warehouse (or alternatively, in flat files.) Data Selection and Pre-analysis are then performed to subset the data. This subset is prepared to improve the quality of the mining results or to overcome limitations in current data mining products. Facilities for doing data selection and pre-analysis are usually provided with many mining tools.

Phase-II – Mining Operations

The second phase of the Data Mining process is the phase where the actual mining takes place. The Data Mining processor accesses the data store, mart, database (flat file or relational) or a warehouse. This access is facilitated through a standard SQL interface. Using a middleware product simplifies the mining of data from multiple sources.

Phase – III – Presentation

The last phase is concerned with the presentation of the information or knowledge discovered in phase II. The phase also completes any residual follow-up action required on the results of phase II. The presentation can be done by the data mining processor or a suitable front-end tool such as the IBM Visualizer. The need for an iterative process can be achieved through querying or through the application of other mining operators on the data discovered in phase II.

3.7 Visualization

Data mining extracts previously unknown information from a database. This includes relationships between variables that are non-intuitive and represent knowledge. The challenge lies in interpreting the knowledge discovered and its conversion into an actionable solution to a business problem. The challenge is accentuated by the fact that the user has no prior clue as to the kind of information or knowledge that would be discovered by the mining system. There are usually many ways to graphically represent a model. The visualizations that are used should be chosen to maximize the value to the viewer. This requires that the system designer understands the viewer's needs and designs the visualization with the end-user in mind.

3.7.1 Orienteering

Orienteering is a family of sports that requires navigational skills using a map and compass to steer from point to point in diverse and usually unfamiliar terrain at a decent clip (Wikipedia). Orienteering is typically accomplished by employing the two major approaches listed below:

    i.   Maps

    ii.   Landmarks

Example - 17

An individual needs to find the location of an office in an unknown city. He has been given instructions to the reach the office. The usual method is to obtain a map showing the details, especially commercial areas, within the city. Once the office address is located on the map, the person would walk along aligning with landmarks such as street names until office address is located. The degree to which an individual would follow the landmark chain or trust the map depends upon the match between the landmarks and the map. It would be reinforced by unexpected matches (as one traverses along the route and comes across landmarks) along the route. The confidence of the individual would be also be dependent on knowledge of the city, previous experience in locating destination using a map as well as the nature of their journey. The combination of a global coordinate system (the map) and the local coordinate system (landmarks along the route) must fit together and must instill confidence as the journey is traversed. The concept of a manifold is relevant in that the global coordinates must be realizable as a combination of local coordinate systems. The following events are mandatory to instill trust in the users of the system:

- Show that nearby paths (small distances in the model) do not lead to widely different ends.
- The effect that different perspectives (change of variables or inclusion probabilities) have on model structure, on demand
- Effect dynamic changes in coloring, shading, edge definition and viewpoint (dynamic dithering).
- Sprinkle known relationships (landmarks) throughout the model landscape.
- Enhanced user interaction

The advantages of this manifold approach include the ability to explore the terrain in an optimal fashion, the ability to reduce the models to an independent coordinate set, and the ability to measure model adequacy in a more natural manner.

3.8   Data Mining Models – The Imperative

The driving forces behind visualizing data mining models can be broken down into two key areas:

i)   Understanding

ii)   Trust

Understanding is undoubtedly the most fundamental motivation behind visualizing the model. Although the simplest way to deal with a data-mining model is to leave the output in the form of a black box, the user will not necessarily gain an understanding of the underlying behavior in which they are interested. This approach would entail a user to perform tasks like finding out potential customers to target for a marketing/sales campaign, but would not enable them to understand the underlying system nor allow them to perform further action with the outputted data.

A better approach to use a data-mining model is to get the user to actually understand what is going on so that they can perform actions directly. Visualizing a model should allow a user to discuss and explain the logic behind the model with colleagues, customers, and other users. To ensure better results it is important to make the end user aware of the logic employed in developing a system.

For example, if the user is responsible for organizing an advertising or promotional campaign, understanding customer demographics is critical to achieve better results. Decisions about where to employ advertising funds are a direct result of understanding data mining models of customer behavior. Unless the output of the data mining system can be understood qualitatively, it would not be of any use. In addition, the model needs to be understood so that the actions that are taken as a result can be justified to others. Understanding involves knowing the context. If the user can understand what has been discovered in the context of their business issues, they will trust it and put it into use. There are two parts to this problem:

i)   Meaningful Visualization of the data mining output.
ii) User interaction with the visualization engine for simplified query resolution

Creative solutions are incorporated into a number of commercial data mining products like Mine Set. Financial indicators like profits, cost and ROI provides users with a sense of context and establish the validity of the results. The simple visual representations of the data mining results allow users to visualize and understand the data mining results. Graphically displaying a decision tree can significantly change the way in which the data mining software is used. Manipulation of the data and viewing the results dynamically allows the user to get a feel of the dynamics, discover unusual patterns and verify their "gut feel". The interactive nature of the visualization engine helps the user fully comprehend the discovered patterns relating to their customers. Users also often require drill through functions so that they can visualize the actual data behind a model (or some portion of the model). Finally, integrating with other decision support tools like OLAP will let users view the data mining results in a manner that they are already using for the purpose of understanding customer behavior. By incorporating interaction into the process, a user will be able to connect the data mining results with his or her customers.

Since data mining relies heavily on training data, it is important to understand the limitations that a given data set puts on the future application of the resulting model. One class of standard visualization tools involves probability density estimation and clustering over the training data. Especially interesting would be regions of state space that are uncommon in the training data yet do not violate known domain constraints. One would tend to trust a model less if it acts more confident when presented with uncommon data as future inputs. For time-series data, visualizing indicators that are not stationery is also important.

Assessing model trustworthiness is typically much more straightforward than the understanding of the model. This is essentially because the former is largely deconstructive while the latter is constructive. A user without a deep understanding of a given model can still employ general domain knowledge to detect that it violates expected qualitative principles. A relevant example would be a model trying to establish a statistical co-relation between shirt sizes and the emotional quotient (EQ).

Domain knowledge is also critical for detecting and cleaning data to avoid common mistakes like the gender of a patient admitted in a hospital for delivery as "Male". If a data-mining model was built using the erroneous data, the anomalies caused by incorrect data entry will skew the resulting model. The role of visualization techniques is to annotate the model structures with domain knowledge that they violate. Assessing the trust of is also closely related to model comparison. It is essential to understand the sensitivity of model predictions and quality, to changes in parameters and/or structure of the given model. The common technique to visualize such sensitivity is to determine the local and global (conditional) probability densities with focus determining whether multiple modes of high probability exist for some parameters and combinations. Such relative measures of trust can be considerably less demanding to formulate than attempts at more absolute measures. However they place special demands on the visualization engine, which must support quick and non-disorientating navigation through neighboring regions in model space.

Statistical summaries of all sorts are also common and useful for gathering insights for assessing model trust. Pair wise scatter-plots and low-dimensional density estimates are especially common. Summaries can be particularly useful for comparing relative trust of two models, by allowing analysis to focus on subsets of features for which their interrelationships differ most significantly between two models. It is often useful to combine summaries with interactive ability to drill-through to the actual data. Many forms of visual summary actually display multiple scales of data along the raw to abstract continuum, making visual drill-through a natural recursive operation.

For example, compressing millions of samples into a compressed chart based on time series facilitates easy navigation of the data extremities within the given time range. Most useful are models that qualify their own trustworthiness to some degree, such as in quantifying the expected variance in the error of their predictions. However such models are rarely deployed since the normal emphasis is on expected case outcomes rather than worst-case performance.

There are important classes of tasks, such as fraud detection for which quantified variance is essential. The standard techniques employed include confidence intervals and probability density estimation. Bounds estimation is another approach that balances the complexity of general probability density estimation and the simplicity of the mean estimation plus variance estimation approach. It is important to consider multiple transformations of the data during visual exploration of the model sensitivities. For example, a model that accurately predicts the internal pressure of an engineering device would also be able to predict related parameters such as oil density or the device power spectrum. These measures of internal consistency provides the most important method to judge the trustworthiness of a model in addition to standard cross validation error estimation. Automated and interactive means of exploring and visualizing the space (and degrees) of inconsistencies a model entails is a particularly important direction for future research on assessing model trustworthiness.

3.9 Model Understandability

It is a well established fact that "A model that can be understood is a model that can be trusted". While statistical methods build some trust in a model by assessing its accuracy, they cannot assess the model's semantic validity or its applicability to the real world. Domain experts can check a data-mining algorithm that uses a human-understandable model easily, providing much needed semantic validity to the model. Unfortunately, users are often forced to trade off accuracy of a model for understandability. Advanced visualization techniques can greatly expand the range of models that can be understood by domain experts, thereby easing the accuracy/understandability trade-off. Three components are essential for understanding a model:

i. *Representation*

Representation refers to the visual form in which the model appears. A good representation displays the model in terms of visual components that are already familiar to the user

ii. *Interaction*

Interaction refers to the ability to perceive the model in a real time basis to facilitate user exploration in a manner akin to machine interaction

iii. *Integration*

Integration refers to the ability to display relationships between the model and alternate views of the data on which it is based. Integration provides the user context

The following section focuses on understanding the classification models. Each of these models provides a unique form of understanding based on representation, interaction, and integration.

The graphical representation should be simple enough to be easily understood, but complete in order to reveal the information present in the model. This is a difficult balance since simplicity usually trades off against completeness. Three dimensional (3D) visualizations have the potential to reveal more information than two-dimensional (2D) visualizations while retaining their simplicity. Navigation lets an individual focus on an element of interest while keeping the rest of the structure in context. It is important to note that the user should be able to navigate through 3D visualization in real time. An image of a 3D scene is merely a 2D projection and is usually more difficult to understand than a scene built in two dimensions. Even with three dimensions, many models still contain far too much information that cannot be displayed easily. The visualization must simplify the representation as it is displayed. The decision tree and decision table visualizers use the principle of hierarchical simplification to present a large amount of information to the user.

Decision trees are easy to understand but can become overwhelmingly large when automatically induced. Only the first few levels of the tree are initially displayed, despite the fact that the tree is extensive. The user can gain a basic understanding of the tree by following the branches of these levels. Additional levels of detail are revealed only when the user navigates to a deeper level, providing more information only as needed.

Using decision tables as a model representation generates a simple but large model. A full decision table theoretically contains the entire dataset, which may be very large. Therefore simplification is essential. A decision table arranges the model into levels based on the importance of each feature in the table. The data is automatically aggregated to provide a summary using only the most important features. When the user desires more information, he can drill down as many levels as needed to answer his question. The visualization automatically changes the aggregation of the data to display the desired level of detail.

While a good representation can greatly aid the user's understanding, in many cases the model contains too much information to provide a representation that is both complete and understandable. In these cases we exploit the brain's ability to reason about cause and effect and let the user interact with the more complex model. Interaction can be thought of as "understanding by doing" as opposed to "understanding by seeing".

Common forms of interaction are interactive classification, interactive model building, drill-up, drill-down, animation, searching, filtering, and level-of-detail manipulation. The fundamental techniques of searching, filtering, drill-up, and drill-down, make the task of finding information hidden within a complex model easier. However, they do not help overall understanding much. More extensive techniques (interactive classification, interactive model building) are required to help the user understand a model that is too complicated to show with a static image or table. These advanced methods aid understanding by visually showing the answer to a user query while maintaining a simplified representation of the model for context.

Beyond interactive classification, interactively guiding the model-building process provides additional control and understanding to the user. The user may suggest splits, perform pruning, or manually construct sections of the tree, providing enhanced context sensitive user understanding of the model. This requires an understanding of the relationship between the model and the underlying data. This necessitates integration of tools with the model. The following techniques are commonly used:

  i)   Drill-through
  ii)   Brushing
  iii) Coordinated visualizations

Drill-through refers to the ability to select a portion of a model and gain access to the original data from which the model was derived. For example, the decision tree visualizer allows selection and drill-through on individual branches of the tree. This will provide access to the original data that was used to construct those branches, leaving out the data represented by other parts of the tree.

Brushing refers to the ability to select pieces of a model and have the selections appear in an alternate representation.

Coordinated visualizations generalize both techniques by screening multiple representations of the same model, combined with representations of the original data. Interactive actions that affect the model also affect the other visualizations. These techniques help users understand how the model relates to the original data. This provides an external context for the model and helps establish semantic validity. As data mining becomes more extensive in industry and as the number of automated techniques employed increases, there is a natural tendency for models to become increasingly complex. It is essential to develop more sophisticated visualization techniques to keep pace with the increasing model complexity.

3.9.1 Visualization Model Comparison

Model comparison necessitates the creation of an appropriate metric for the models under consideration. To visualize the model comparison, these metrics must be visually interpretable by a human observer. The first step is to create a mapping of the entire modeling process. The second step is to map this process to the human visual space.

It is important to recognize that the word "model" can have several levels of meaning. Common usage often associates the word model with the data modeling process. For example, one might talk of applying a neural network model to a particular problem. In this case, the word model refers to the generic type of model known as a neural network. Another use of the word model is associated with the end result of the modeling process. A model based on the neural network could include a specific set of weights, topology, and node types that produces an output given a set of inputs. In still another use, the word model refers to the input-output mapping associated with a "black-box." Such a mapping necessarily places emphasis on careful identification of the input and output spaces.

3.9.2 Input/Output Mappings

The input-output approach to model comparison simply considers the mapping from a defined input space to a defined output space. For example, one might consider a specific 1-gigabyte database with twenty-five variables (columns). The input space is simply the Cartesian product of the database's twenty-five variables. Any actions inside the model, such as creation of new variables, are hidden in the "black-box" and are not interpreted. At the end of the modeling process, an output is generated. This output could be a number, a prioritized list or even a set of rules about the system. The crucial issue is that we can define the output space in some consistent manner to derive an input to output mapping.

It is the space generated by the mappings that is of primary importance to the model comparison. For most applications the mapping space will be well defined once the input and output spaces are well defined. For example, two classifiers could be described by a set of input/output pairs, such as (tes1, class A), (tes2, class B), etc. The comparison metric could then be defined on these pairs as a count of the number differing, or GINI indices, or classification cost, etc. The resulting set of pairs could be visualized by simple plotting of points on a 2D graph. The two models could be indexed by coloring or symbol codes. Alternately one could focus on the difference between each model directly and plot the result.

3.9.3 Algorithmic Approach

A reasonable way to approach the model comparison problem is to adopt the view of a model as static algorithm. For example, a neural network model and an adaptive nonlinear regression model might be compared. These models would be expressed as a series of algorithmic steps. Each model's algorithm could then be analyzed by standard methods for measurement of algorithmic performance such as complexity, finite word length and stability. The investigator could also include measures on the physical implementation of the algorithm such as computation time, or computation size. Using these metrics the visualization could take the form of bar charts, graph plotting the difference between the two models on each metric or color/symbol encoding. Each comparison would be for a static snapshot while dynamic behavior would be illustrated through a series of snapshots in a manner analogous to a motion picture.

3.9.4 Process Comparison

The view of a model as a process is perhaps the most ill defined and the most intractable of the three views. The sheer complexity makes it the most important view for the application of visualization. The modeling process includes methods, users, database, support resources and constraints such as knowledge, time and analysis implementation. For the sake of simplicity the scope can be limited based on the assumption that the model comparison is being applied for a single user on a single database over a short time period. This facilitates the exclusion of user differences, database differences, and knowledge differences within the model. For most SMEs the implementation and the analysis are not separable hence an additional assumption that this issue can be ignored as well has to be made. These assumptions facilitate the comparison of the modeling method and implementation simultaneously.

These could be different general methods such as neural networks versus tree-based classifiers, or they could be different levels of sophistication within a class of models such as CART versus CHAID tree-structures. It needs to be noted that the main focus is on the modeling process, and not its input/output or algorithmic structure. Such a situation permits reasonable definition of metrics. For example, the running time could be such a metric, or the interpretability of instructions, or the number of tuning parameters that must be chosen by the user at run-time. The key here is that these metrics must be tailored to the user who is the target of the application. The process comparison approach focuses on the user needs and perceptions as opposed to the input-output view that focused on the spaces and the algorithmic that was based on the properties of the algorithm independent of the user.

The chosen set of metrics should be able to project the distances between models in each of the defined metrics using a variety of visual display techniques including Color or symbol coding. There will be atleast one metric defined per user during the model-building process. However it is improbable that a single set of metrics can satisfy individual requirements. Hence it is more useful to establish sound metrics while designing methods to establish them in new situations. It is pertinent to note that metrics that will be chosen by a research scholar would be very different from those chosen by a business user. The properties of good set of metrics, for the modeling process are as listed:

i)   Provide direct risk/benefit analysis to the user.
ii)   Evaluate the sensitivity to model input and assumptions
iii) Provide auditing facility
iv)   Dynamic in nature
v)   Facilitate summarization
vi)   Provide reference to landmarks and markers

Some aspects of the visualization process will take on added importance. One such aspect is the sequential behavior of the modeling process. For example, it is common to plot frequently the updated fit between the data and the model predictions as a neural network learns. A human being will probably give more trust to a method that mimics their own learning behavior (A learning curve which starts with a few isolated details, then grows quickly to broad generalizations and then makes only incremental gains after that in the typical "S" shape). Unstable behavior or large swings should count against the modeling process.

Another aspect of importance should a visual track of the sensitivity of the modeling process to small changes in the data and modeling process parameters. For example, one might make several random starts with different random weights in a neural network model. These should be plotted versus one another showing their convergence patterns, again perhaps against a theoretical S-shaped convergence.

The model must also be auditable, meaning that inquiries may be made at any reasonable place in the modeling process. In case of a neural network there should exist a facility to interrupt and examine individual weights at any step in the modeling process. In as similar fashion in case of a tree-based model there should be a facility to view the sub trees as required. In an ideal scenario there could be several scales in which this interruption could occur. Since most humans operate on a system of local and global coordinates it will be important to be able to supplement the visualizations with markers and a general map structure.

For example – There can be a direct comparison between two neural nets with different structures. However it would be effective to have the same distances plotted for another method with which the user is familiar (Discriminant analysis) even if that method is inadequate. If the same model could be used on a known input, the user could establish trust with the new results. It might also be useful to have simultaneously a detailed and a summarized model displayed. For example, the full tree-based classifier might have thirty two branches, but the summarized tree might show the broad limbs only. In case if the output is a rule, it would be extremely useful to drive (through logical manipulation) other results or statements of results, as a test of reasonableness.

3.10 Summary

Data mining offers business enterprises the ability to discover hidden patterns in their data that can provide tangible financial benefits. These patterns provide insights to customer behavior and help orient products and services in tune with market trends. The advent of parallel processing and new processing technologies enable customers to capitalize on the benefits of data mining more effectively than had been possible previously.

One of the essential factors for the success of relational databases and SQL is the existence of a well-founded mathematical models and language. OLAP and data mining are integral parts of any decision support process. Traditionally most OLAP systems have focused on providing access to multi-dimensional data, while data mining systems have dealt with "influence analysis" of data along a single dimension. OLAP and data mining should not be considered as separate pillars of the decision support framework, but should be fully merged, as they are inherently related activities that reinforce each other. Decision support applications must consider data mining within multiple dimensions while OLAP systems need to focus on discovery as much as on access. Data mining, the extraction of hidden predictive information from large databases, has a high potential to help modern day service oriented organizations by predicting future trends and behaviors thereby allowing them to make proactive, knowledge-driven decisions.

3.11 Exercise Questions

1. Briefly explain the commonly employed Data Mining techniques.
2. Explain the architecture of a Data Mining system.
3. What is meant by influence domains?
4. Discuss the commonly employed data mining models.
5. Mention some of the potential applications of data mining.
6. List down the differences between verification and discovery in a Decision Support System.
7. What are the key phases of the Data Mining Repository Framework? Explain the significance of each.
8. What are the essential characteristics of a well-designed model?
9. Discuss some of the visualization techniques adopted by data mining systems.

Chapter Objectives

The objectives of this chapter are:

- *To highlight the relationship between data mines and data warehouses.*
- *To introduce the different data analysis techniques*
- *To present the architecture of Enterprise Decision Support Systems*
- *To provide an understanding of the various methods of employing data mining techniques within a data warehouse*

Chapter 4

DATA MINES FOR DATA WAREHOUSES

4.1 Introduction

Historically data mining was viewed as a "subset" of the activities associated with the warehouse. However it is important to note and understand that data warehousing are two different sides of a coin. A data warehouse is the optimal source for the data to be mined while data mining is a separate discipline that is employed to discover patterns in the underlying dataset. Data mining significantly influences the design and implementation of large data warehouses. The earlier approach was to build a data warehouse first and later apply mining tools to extract information from the warehouse. A much better way is to "sandwich" the warehousing effort between two layers of mining, thus understanding the data before warehousing it. This concept is illustrated in the figure 4.1 (Parsaye Kamran, 1995). This chapter explores the three strategies for data mining in the context of a data warehouse. The requirements different data structures, computational processes that enable a data mining system to cater to differing group of users are also discussed.

Figure 4.1 – Data Mining Process

Although warehousing and mining are undoubtedly related activities and can reinforce each other, data mining requires different data structures, computational processes and caters to a different group of users than the typical warehouse. One needs to carefully separate these processes and understand how they differ in order to use them effectively. Similar to a Data Mart there could also exist structures referred to as Data Mines, that are built specifically designed to help in mining data. The Data Mine is a repository that can either co-exist with, or be distinct from the data warehouse. The 'Sandwich Paradigm', as discussed above, ensures that the Warehouse and the Mine work in unison.

4.2 Storage & Analysis

The purpose of most warehouses is to bring together large amounts of historical data from several sources and to facilitate decision support. The figure 4.2 illustrates the block diagram of a Decision Support System (DSS) (Datawarehousing.com, 1997).

Figure 4.2 – Structure of a Decision Support System

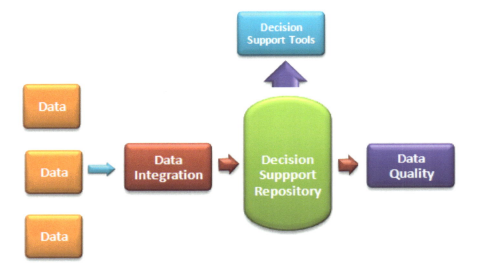

The repository may have distinct components such as the warehouse and the data mine. The activities performed on a large corporate data repositories are usually diverse and includes distinct tasks such as query and reporting, multi-dimensional analysis and data mining. These tasks naturally break into separate user groups, as well as distinct computational processes (Datawarehousing.com, 1997).

Access and analysis operate on different computational spaces with additional "derived spaces" for information processing and handling. Data access operations such as query and reporting happen with the data space while OLAP operates within the multi-dimensional space, data mining takes place in the Influence Space. The four spaces, which form the basis of decision support, are shown in Figure 4.3. They are the spaces for data, aggregation, influence and variation. A fifth space based on geographic relationships may also be used for some analyses. A data warehouse is thus the natural place for storing the "data space". It is where the base level data elements are stored so that they could be later analyzed to deliver information. The analysis dealing with the "influence space" is performed within the Data Mine.

Figure 4.3 – Spaces within a Decision Support System

The questions posed to these spaces are inherently different. Some questions such as "what influences sales?" are almost impossible to answer "directly" from the data space. Moreover, the derived spaces are often so large that they cannot be fully pre-computed and stored like the data space, e.g. one cannot easily pre-compute all influence factors within a large database beforehand. Hence, often on has to rely on a partial pre-computation of these spaces, with further dynamic computations performed for providing answers to specific queries (Datawarehousing.com, 1997).

The data space includes all the information contained in the other spaces but in a less refined form. It forms the basis for the derivation of the other spaces.

However, once computed these become real spaces in their own right. Hence the data space is build initially and the other spaces are derived from it. They can also serve as the basis for deriving hybrid spaces that can influence analysis on aggregations and/or variations. These hybrid spaces deliver highly refined and usable information from the raw data stored within the warehouse.

In the process of analysis, the data space often needs to be enriched with additional semantics by adding information about hierarchies and periodic behavior. This additional semantics goes beyond the simple relational model, but often helps the user. For instance, {month, quarter, year} and {city, state, country} form natural hierarchies which the simple relational model ignores. By adding such semantics to the OLAP space one can provide a good deal of additional benefit to the user. While the OLAP space mostly deals with the computation of numeric values, the influence space has a "logical nature". It deals with the influence of specific groups of items on the others.

The information within the "influence space" is typically very abstract and represents knowledge Hence this space is regarded as the most important among all the spaces that are generated to support a Data Mine. Information and Knowledge are the most valuable commodities in the modern world, and with the increasing complexity of business enterprises, the information obtained by data mining can be exponentially more valuable than any other asset.

It should, however, be noted that the size of the influence space and the number of logical combinations of influence factors can be extremely large, making it very hard to pre-compute this space. Restricting this to a smaller space is not a viable option since the goal is to find unexpected patterns and the four fields that are excluded may hold the key to the problem. Hence discovery is inherently a very dynamic process and often leads to a chain reaction.

4.3 Exploratory and Confirmatory Analyses

Data mining can be thought of as a decision support process that helps in the search for patterns of information in data. This search maybe manually initiated by a user, e.g. running a query, or may be assisted by smart programs that automatically search the database to uncover significant patterns. This process is referred to as "discovery". Discovery is the process of scanning a database to find hidden patterns without a predetermined idea or hypothesis (es) about what the patterns may be. In other words, the program takes the initiative in finding what the interesting patterns are, without the user thinking of the relevant questions first. In large databases, there are so many patterns, that a user can never practically think of the right questions to ask. This aspect distinguishes this space from the others. From a statistical perspective, there are two types of analyses:

(i) **Confirmatory Analysis**

Confirmatory analysis is based on the acceptance or rejection of a hypothesis (es) using inferential statistical reasoning. However lack of a concrete hypothesis (es) can be a bottleneck for this type of analysis.

(ii) **Exploratory Analysis.**

Exploratory Analysis aims to find suitable hypothesis (es) to confirm or reject. Automatic discovery simplifies the process of exploratory data analysis, allowing unskilled analysts to explore very large datasets much more effectively.

A data warehouse may be a suitable place for performing confirmatory analysis and exploring at the data space. However it is not suited for performing exploratory analysis due to the unexpected nature of the queries posed to the data. The natural place for exploratory analysis is a Data Mine as opposed to a Data warehouse.

4.4 Warehouse Patterns

The dual concept of a large warehouse and meaningful patterns interact in a seemingly contradictory way. On one hand, the larger a warehouse, the richer its pattern content, i.e. as the warehouse grows it includes more patterns. On the other hand, after a point, if a large portion of the warehouse is analyzed, patterns from different data segments begin to dilute each other and the number of useful patterns begins to decrease

The basic idea is illustrated in Figure 4.4. The following examples drives home the concept.

Example 18

Consider a Data Warehouse designed for a large bank with a national presence. The warehouse includes the details of the bank's customers including their accounts and their marketing/promotional campaigns among others. There can be several business objectives for mining this data, including analyzing the effect of promotional campaigns, means of achieving higher customer retention, profitability and risk assessments. It may be noted that each of the mentioned activities are distinct business tasks and it mandates individual analysis. As a result data mining exercises needs to be performed separately with require different data structures, association analyses and clustering.

The analysis of the promotional campaign should however not be performed on the entire warehouse. The bank may have undertaken 30 different marketing campaigns over the years, and these campaigns will have usually involved different products and different customer segments including products that would have been discontinued. In order to understand and analyze the projected response to a promotional event each of the campaigns (or a group of campaigns) have to considered separately since each campaign would involve patterns with distinct signatures. Mixing the analyses into one data mining exercise will simply dilute the differences between these signatures besides the fact that most of the campaigns distinct and integrating them may not be appropriate option. This necessitates having separate "Analysis Session" for each group of campaigns. The following example illustrates the concepts above concept.

Example 19

It is assumed that customers who are over 40 years old and have more than 2 children have a high response rate to credit card promotions. Further it is also assumed that customers who are less than 40 years old and have only 1 child are good prospects for opening new children savings accounts. If the campaigns mentioned above are combined within the same data mining study with a view of finding out customers who have a high response rate, these two patterns will dilute each other.

One could formulate a rule that separates these campaigns and still display the patterns. However in a large warehouse there would numerous rules that will overwhelm the user. Large amounts of conditional segment information may reveal smaller patterns within the warehouse. An example could be the standard 'If... Then' statements - "If Campaign=PM22 and ... Then..." However, in a large warehouse, there are so many of these statements that a user will be overloaded with them. The best way to resolve this issue is to analyze each group of campaigns separately.

Figure 4.4 – Data Warehouse Patterns

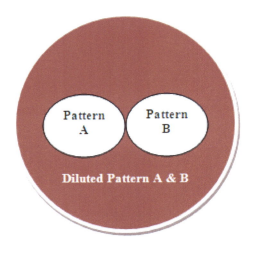

Diluted Pattern A & B

The need for segmentation is even clearer in case of predictive modeling. While attempting to predict the response to a new campaign, it simply does not make sense to base the predictions on all previous campaigns that have ever taken place, but on those campaigns that are most similar to the one being considered. For instance, responses to campaigns for savings account for a new branch of a bank may have little bearing on responses to campaigns for a new credit card or a home finance. In this case, the paradox of the warehouse patterns comes into play in that by considering more data, the accuracy is lost. This is due to the fact that some of the data is not relevant to the task being considered. The analysis of the campaigns will have no bearing on the key indicators that are common to all the campaigns being considered. If a pattern holds strongly enough in the entire database, it will also hold in the segments. For instance, if the people with more than 3 children never respond to campaigns, this fact will also be true in each individual campaign.

As another example, consider a vehicle warranty database of an automobile assembling corporation. In order to find patterns for customer claims it is essential to store details of each claim in a large data warehouse. However it does not make sense to analyze the entire warehouse at the same time since in practice cars are built at different plants, different models of cars use different parts and some parts may be discontinued. Moreover, over the course of years the parts used in cars change, hence the analysis of the entire warehouse may provide less information than the analysis of a part of the warehouse. In practice it would be better to analyze the claims for a given model year for cars built at a given plant. This forms the basis of a segmentation task. Analyzing the warehouse in its entirety would reduce the number of useful patterns that are being generated. Generally it does not make sense to analyze the entire warehouse since patterns are lost through dilution. To find useful patterns in a large warehouse a segment (as opposed to a sample) of data that fits a business objective has to be selected and prepared for analysis as a precursor to the data mining operation. Observing the entire data set together often hides the patterns, since the factors that apply to distinct business objectives often dilute each other.

4.5   Sampling and Summarization

Sampling is a quick fix to faster data analysis. However the end results are often less than desirable. Sampling was used within statistics because it was so difficult to have access to an entire population, e.g. one could not interview a million people, or one could not have access to a million manufactured components. Hence, sampling methods were developed to allow rough calculations about some of the characteristics of the population without access to the entire population. Segmentation is inherently a different task from sampling. Segmentation allows one to focus on a subset of the data (e.g. one model year for a car, or one campaign), sharpening the focus of the analysis. Sampling leads to loss of data since it takes into account only a random subset of data while discarding the other data available.

The hardware technology for storing and analyzing large datasets provide an unprecedented opportunity for observing historical patterns by making more data accessible for analysis. At times it may be tempting to analyze a smaller subset of data. For e.g. If the analysis of a 100,000,000 record retail database is required it may be tempting to analyze a 100,000 record sample. However sampling will almost always result in a loss of information, in particular with respect to data fields with a large number of non-numeric values. The following example illustrates this concept.

Example 20

Consider a warehouse of 1,000 products and 500 stores. There are half a million combinations of how a product sells in each store. However, how one product sells in a store is of little interest compared to how products "sell together" in each store. This is commonly referred to as Market Basket Analysis. There are 500 million possible combinations possible and a 100,000 record sample is a small fraction of this population. Hence the sample will be a really "rough" representation of the data, and will ignore key pieces of information. In using a small sample it may be prudent to ignore the product column   Hence sampling a large warehouse for analysis almost defeats the purpose of having all the data stored within the database.

In addition to sampling, summarization may be used to reduce data sizes. However summarization also can cause problems. The summarization of the same dataset with two sampling or summarization methods may result in the same result, and the summarization of the same data set with two methods may produce two different results. The following example illustrates how information loss and information distortion can take place through summarization.

Example 21

Consider a retail warehouse where the weekday (Monday to Saturday) sales are exceptionally low for some stores, while weekend (Sunday) sales are exceptionally high for others. The summarization of daily sales data to weekly amounts will totally obscure the fact that weekdays are "loss making", while weekends are "profitable" for some stores. In other words, key pieces of information are often lost through summarization and cannot be recovered for further analysis.

Sampling is generally recommended to get a general feeling for the data, and in such cases, one would recommend having several samples and comparing them. Sampling is only resorted to when the computing power is not sufficient to manage the task at hand within a given time frame. In some cases, segmentation alone will not provide the required answers and it may require the analysis of some of the overall database characteristics. These cases however do not necessitate a full exploratory analysis and may only involve a simple comparison of some of the distributions within the warehouse with those within the Data Mine. An affinity or market basket analysis would require the comparison of two products that sell together in all stores as compared to how they sell together within specific clusters of stores analyzed within a Data Mine.

A lot of these computations may be performed routinely when data is refreshed within the warehouse, and the overall distributions may be kept for such comparisons. Some cases may require the application of segmented affinity analysis on the entire warehouse in order to discover the optimal method to segment the data. Thus specific operations on the entire warehouse are performed first in order to guide the segmentation process. Hence whenever there is a requirement to view a database in its entirety, it has to be done selectively and with proper planning.

4.6 Analysis Session

A Data Mine uses a segment (and not a sample) of data from a warehouse (or other related sources) to perform discovery or prediction. The process of mining this data segment is referred to as an Analysis Session. The task could be predicting the response to a proposed direct mail campaign by analyzing previous campaigns for similar products, or may involve data concerning the variation of customer retention over various geographic regions pan India. The analysis session can be either:

   i.   Structured Session

ii.   Unstructured Session

A structured session is a formal activity which initiates with a specific task like the profitability analysis of customer segments or products. Structured sessions are often performed in a routine manner similar to the quarterly analysis of costs, revenues or expenses for trending, forecasting or demand estimation segmented market wise. It may also involve the search for unusual transactions over a specified time period. A structured analysis session usually takes the following three forms:

i.   Discovery

ii.   Prediction

iii. Forensic Analysis

An unstructured session is a one where the user wanders around without a goal, hoping to uncover something of interest by serendipity or by help from an exploration agent. This type of abstract search usually uncovers some very wild facts hidden in the data. The mine is a natural place for this activity because the unexpected nature of queries may interfere with the more routine tasks for which the warehouse was designed, e.g. looking up the history of a specific claim. The data in the Data Mine often needs to be enriched with aggregations which are additional elements added to the data. The business analysis dictates how these aggregations are built. For instance, one might require viewing the information regarding the number of credit cards a customer has as an item or the volume of transactions the customer has had or the number of motor claims filed by a customer. These aggregations enrich the data and co-exist with the atomic level data in the mine.

4.7   Enterprise Decision Support Systems

There are three separate components to an enterprise-wide decisions support system:

(i)   Data Warehouse

The Warehouse is the repository for the corporate data. The data volumes are usually very high and the designs are commonly based on star-schemas, snow-flakes or highly normalized data structures

(ii)   Data Mart

The Data Mart is a repository of departmental and the various external data items that are usually added to the mart. The data volumes are usually 15% to 30% of the warehouse size. These databases are also usually either based on star-schemas or are in a normalized form. They mostly deal with the data space, but at times some multi-dimensional analysis is performed.

(iii)   Data Mine

The Data Mine is an area where the data is re-organized for analysis and information is extracted from the data. The data volumes here are similar to a Data Mart. However the data is much more richly structured and is not restricted to departmental groupings. The data maps to specific business objectives and is analyzed for the purpose of information extraction.

While the data structures used within the warehouse and the mart may be similar, the data structures used within the Data Mine are significantly different. The Data Mine differs from the Data warehouse not just in the size of data it manages, but also in the structure of the data. This is due to the fact the mine contains additional external data not found within the warehouse.

The data mining architecture is not conducive to the standard principles of data structuring that are applicable to a database or a data warehouse. The two key approaches to data structuring within warehouses are normalization and star-schema families, which include snowflake schemas. Normalization is a methodology for data structuring for OLTP applications. However the limitations of normalization theory become evident when it is applied to dimensional analysis for decision support. This led to the development of star schemas and databases engines. While normalization theory deals with the data space, star schemas deal with the aggregation space. Star schemas may be suitable for dimensional analysis in the aggregation space but they are not ideal for data mining within the influence space since the structure of this space is logical, and not arithmetic or polynomial. The data structures in the Data Mine need to be both de-normalized and super-dimensional.

4.8　Data Mining & Warehousing

The data mine is distinct from the data warehouse and can exist in three basic forms:

i.　　A set of conceptual views (Above the warehouse)

ii.　　A separate repository (Besides the warehouse)

iii.　　A distinct set of resources (Within the warehouse)

Data mining "above the warehouse" provides a minimal architecture for the discovery and analysis. It is suitable only in cases where data mining is not a key objective for the warehouse. In this approach, as shown in Figure 4.5, SQL statements are used to build a set of conceptual views above the warehouse tables. Additional external data from other tables may be merged as part of the views.

Figure 4.5 – Data Mining above the Warehouse

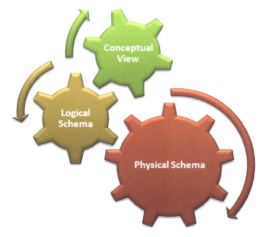

The views built above the warehouse can be materialized (i.e. saved t as new tables). However if the views are not of significant size, then serious data mining cannot take place. However, if the views are of a significant size, then without materialization the effort in repeatedly computing them will require very large amounts of processing power. In some cases it may significantly affect the availability of the warehouse resources while interfering with other applications during index retrievals.

On the other hand, if the views are of a significant size and they are materialized, the form would not be referred to as data mining "above" the warehouse and will constitute a disorganized form of data mining within the warehouse. If the views are materialized, the third approach will almost always work better, because it can utilize a suitable data distribution approach and a specific processor allocation strategy while employing different data structures for data mining. Without these precautions, the number of potential pitfalls increases rapidly, leading to loss of performance as well as functionality. Hence data mining above the warehouse should be restricted to applications in which data mining is not a key objective.

In most cases, data mining is effectively performed beside the warehouse, with data structures that lend themselves to detailed analyses. In most cases additional data suitable for the analyses is integrated with the warehoused data in order to perform specific analyses for focused business needs. The concept of data mining beside the warehouse fits well within the context of three-level computing and resembles the three-tiered client server architecture. Within this architecture, the first tier client interacts with a middle-tier server that also interacts with a third tier larger system. While in three-tiered client-server systems the interaction between layers 2 and 3 is on-going, in a three-level computing system, most of the interaction is between the client and a "specialized server" which occasionally accesses a server that holds very large amounts of data, and is surrounded by a number of specialized servers that interact with the clients. The overall architecture for data mining beside the warehouse is shown in Figure 4.6. The process of data migration and fusion populates a data warehouse with large amounts of historical data. The data structures used within the warehouse may be either normalized or members of the star schema family. However, the data schemas for the Data Mine will be completely different. Query and reporting tools, as well as other applications utilizing traditional database index structures may directly access the warehouse. However, detailed analyses such as discovery and prediction are not performed within the warehouse since they do not relate to the data space. Instead these activities are performed in the Data Mine, with data structures suitable for data mining.

Figure 4.6 – Data Mining besides the Warehouse

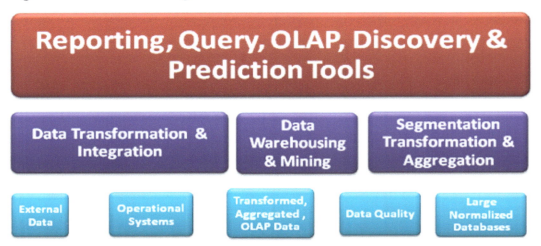

Data mining beside the warehouse overcomes and skirts several known issues in one go. To begin with, it allows data mining to be done with the right data structures, avoiding the problems associated with the structures of the data space. Moreover, the paradox of warehouse patterns can be avoided by selecting specific data segments, corresponding to specific business objectives. The interactive exploratory analyses that are often performed in the Data Mine, with random searches through the data, no longer interfere with the warehouse resources responsible for routine processes such as query and reporting. Different business departments can use their own data mines that address their specific needs. The data is subsequently moved from a large warehouse to the mine, is restructured during the transformation and is analyzed. It is, however, important to design the transfer and transformation methods carefully, in order to allow for optimal refresh methods that require minimal computing. For instance as new data is introduced into the Data Mine the over-head for re-aggregation should be minimized.

In some cases, where the warehouse is a very large as in case of massively parallel processing (MPP) computers a data mine may actually reside as a separate repository within the large warehouse. As shown in Figure 4.7, this is very similar to a data mine beside the warehouse, where the mine uses a portion of the physical warehouse, but is independent of the warehouse structures.

Figure 4.7 – Data Mining within the Warehouse

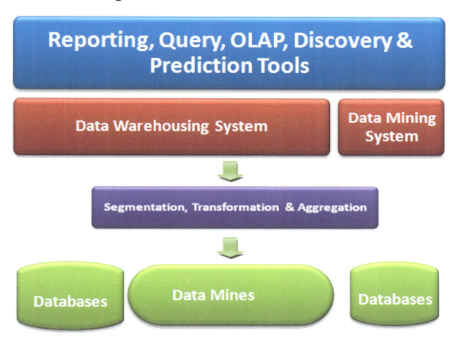

In such scenarios, the disk apace and the processors for the Data Mine are specifically allocated and separately managed. For example on a machine with 32 processors the disk space for the data mine is separately allocated on 8 of the 32 nodes and 8 processors are dedicated to data mining, while the other 24 processors manage the rest of the warehouse. As per requirement additional processing capability may be made available for data mining. The above functionality is suitable for a centralized architecture and supports scalability. However in practice it usually leads to loss of flexibility, without providing any significant benefits for data mining. The key point is that the likelihood of serving the needs of many people within the data space is much higher than the likelihood of serving their needs within the multi-dimensional and influence spaces. While the data elements may be almost the same for several departments, the dimensions, the influence relationships and the predictive models needed will vary far more than their simple data needs. While the design of the data space may be subject to compromises to please the various user groups, there should be no compromises in design of the data mine where serious and detailed analyses take place. The data mine should be optimized to deliver effective results by focusing on specific business needs, because influence analysis is so much harder than data access.

4.9 Stand-Alone Data Mines

A data mine may exist without a warehouse. This usually happens when a business unit within an organization needs to get results quickly and cannot accommodate the time delay to build a very large corporate warehouse. A stand-alone data mine is the best way to guide the data warehouse design process. Often, a significant portion of the business benefits from the system are to be obtained from the data mine, and the horizontal and vertical prototypes built will ensure that the eventual system will conform to the implicit needs of the user. A key issue of concern for managing a stand-alone data mine is data fusion and quality management. These are problems that a large warehouse faces and dealing with them in the context of a data mine is not much more difficult. However they need to be handled with a great deal of care and attention. The need for stand-alone Data Mines usually arises when large warehousing projects have to deal with large amounts of distinct data that are needed to meet the requirements of different departments. Thus stand-alone data mines deployed prior to the warehouse not only provide for the needs of user groups, but also deliver significant business benefits.

The following section illustrates a methodology for using data mining to assist data warehouse development and how the warehousing effort can be sandwiched between two layers of data mining to avoid badly defined storage architecture with data structures that will not easily lend themselves to analysis.

4.10 The Sandwich Paradigm

The Data Dump Paradigm is a two-step linear paradigm that conveniently separates the decision support effort from the data warehousing effort. In this paradigm, the data is moved onto the warehouse initially and subsequently analyzed. However the issues begin to surface post migration since the data was not well understood. The solution provided by the Sandwich Paradigm is logical and involves the pre-analysis of data before it is moved into the Data Warehouse.

Figure 4.8 – Data Dump

As shown in Figure 4.8, the conventional process of data mining consists of two steps:

    i.   Data Warehousing
    ii.   Data Mining

The Sandwich Paradigm however employs three steps:

    i.   Data Pre-mining
    ii.   Data Warehousing
    iii.   Data Mining

The data warehousing effort is sandwiched between two layers of data mining. The first mining layer helps in determining the contents of the warehouse while the second layer helps in in-depth data analysis. The pre-analysis of the data to be moved into the Data Warehouse is done using suitable approaches including Concentric Design, and by Pre-Mining with Vertical and Horizontal Prototypes.

4.11 Concentric Design

Concentric Design is an approach that is commonly associated with the Sandwich Paradigm. The basic idea of a Concentric Design is similar to the camera "zoom" function, wherein one can change the resolution of an image as desired. If we focus on one piece of the picture and try to determine exactly what each part of the picture is, recognition becomes difficult. Similarly, in data warehousing premature assumptions are made without prototyping then the assumptions would have to be frequently reworked. In practice, revising the assumption is very expensive in a large-scale project. The different pieces of the picture should become clearer in parallel, and these different pieces all influence each other in how they fit together.

The traditional waterfall model assumes that software design and development is a fairly orderly succession of (possibly overlapping) stages. The waterfall is a linear model of development, which assumes that there is a sequencing of stages through which development must pass. The real shortcomings of traditional linear development lie in: the lack of feedback throughout the design process, and early commitment to ideas that must later be abandoned. Concentric Design is more appropriate to the demands and uncertainties of large-scale warehouse development.

The feedback provided through prototyping is essential to Concentric Design. Prototyping allows us to test the key aspects of a system before it is completely built. Mistakes or faulty assumptions can be subsequently corrected. Concentric Design involves building a first level horizontal prototype to illustrate the 'Look and Feel' of the system. The prototype is constructed with the same fields as the eventual database but with fewer records. SQL transparency is used to evolve the same schemas to the eventual warehouse. This is accompanied by a vertical prototype which is instrumental in measuring system performance.

4.12 Pre-Mining and Prototyping

Pre-mining refers to the process of acquiring a basic understanding of the data prior to warehousing. In this process data is premined and prototyped, followed by additional analysis to validate the design and data content. Prototypes may be categorized as listed below (Information Discovery Inc: 1994):

i.   **Horizontal Prototypes**

   Horizontal prototypes depict the overall functionality of the system; e.g., the overall look and feel, without delving into too much detail at any level.

ii. **Vertical Prototypes**

   Vertical prototypes focus on just one specific detail; e.g., the performance on a specific type of query.

The distinction between horizontal and vertical prototypes is similar to the difference between breadth-first and depth-first search within a tree structure. Horizontal prototypes test the general structure of the overall design, while vertical prototypes test the details of specific functions. The use of horizontal and vertical prototypes needs to be balanced within a prototyping plan.

Prototypes are essential since they help demonstrate basic features (and possible shortcomings) of a warehouse design. After a prototype has been constructed, it can often be extended to a fully functional system while its basic structure is preserved. It is generally considered that a prototype has succeeded if its structure is preserved in the final system. There are two ways of employing prototypes. One can either discard the prototype or evolve it. Once the decision to extend rather than discard a prototype is made it really becomes an early version of the eventual application. To understand the use of prototypes, one needs to figure the overall structure of a data warehousing effort, as illustrated in Figure 4.9.

Figure 4.9 – Structure of a Data Warehouse

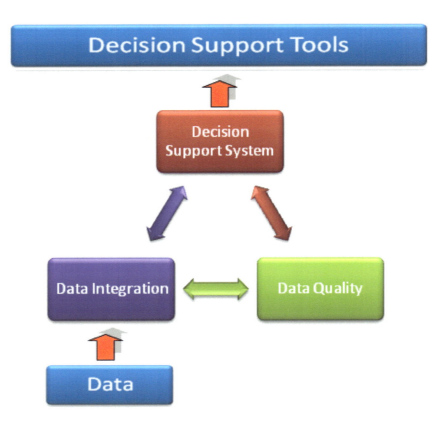

As illustrated in the figure above the data is obtained from multiple sources and is merged within the warehouse. The quality of the data is checked during fusion time and within the warehouse. A good approach to implementing the warehouse is to evolve the system in two or three stages as mentioned below (Information Discovery Inc: 1994):

Stage I

In the first stage of development, the schemas and fields are prototyped on a sample database with fewer records. In this way, modifications to the schema are more easily managed. Given the transparency of SQL, this is a very cost effective activity. The first stage creates a horizontal prototype of the system with a view of obtaining user feedback. A number of vertical prototypes are built in parallel to determine the system bottlenecks and response times and the types of data required and desired by the users are confirmed. This requires the acquisition of additional data, modification of the current schemas while providing a first glance at the quality of the data.

Stage – II

The second stage focuses on performance tuning based on the access trends of users, as well as information tool refinements. This stage determines whether the performance bottlenecks identified in stage one can be easily remedied with the introduction of additional hardware components or if the problems are inherent in the design. Moreover, based on user feedback, additional access and analysis tools are provided and the design is modified. A substantial amount of data is used in this stage.

Concentric Design thus allows us to carefully determine the usability and access patterns of the users and provide them with the best system in the long run. The key elements in Horizontal Prototyping are:

i.   Identify 3 key user groups
ii.   Identify the data sources to be merged
iii. Mine a sample from each data source on its own
iv.   Design first level schemas with from the sample obtained in the previous step
v.   Share the results of the sample obtained in step 3 with some users
vi.   Merge sample data from each source in a horizontal prototype
vii. Mine the merged sample in several dimensions
viii. Share the results of the sample obtained in step 7 with users and adjust horizontal prototype
ix.   Obtain first level user feedback from the vertical prototype
x.   Adjust assumptions, and rework schemas accordingly

The following are the steps required for Vertical Prototyping:

i.   Select suitable test criteria for portions of the system for performance testing, based on user needs and feedback in step 9 above
ii.   Gather reasonable amounts of data for these portions, and perform the tests
iii. Analyze performance with careful scale-up measures for larger datasets

iv. Modify schemas of step 4 or step 10 above, based on the results obtained in the previous step

v. Reiterate these steps as needed, until users are satisfied with the prototype

The selection of suitable samples is essential for the success of the prototypes. The key components and landmarks for the system include the user groups and the tool functionality components, as well as specific response times.

4.13 User Groups

One of the key goals in building a data warehouse is the reduction of the reliance on intermediaries for information access. The system allows end-users to graphically interact and perform queries, obtain graphs and reports without the need for a programmer. The analysis and access tools are what the users see and use. They greatly impact the user's perception, satisfaction and level of success with the system. Typically the system has three distinct groups of users, supported by programmers and database administrators, as illustrated in Figure 4.10.

One of the major users of the information and knowledge generated through mining of databases are the executives or management team within business enterprises. This category of users does not perform any development activities and usually interact with the system using graphical or point-and-click interfaces.

Figure 4.10 – User Groups

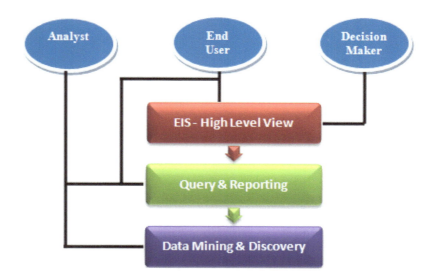

The second classes of users handle the mining interface for their managers and are familiar with word processing and spreadsheet packages. The next classes of users are analysts who mine the data bases for pattern and knowledge discovery. The data warehouse supports each of these groups. However it is to be noted that these users have varied requirements for tools like querying & reporting, executive information processing and data mining (Information Discovery Inc: 1994).

4.14 Tools Classification

Data mining is a decision support process that enables the search and identification of patterns of information within data stores. This search may be initiated by the user by querying or may be assisted smart programs that automatically searches the database for the user and finds significant patterns. Once the information is found, it needs to be presented in a suitable form, with graphs, reports, etc. Data Mining by discovery is the process of looking in a database to find hidden patterns without a predetermined idea or hypothesis about what the patterns may be. In other words, the program takes the initiative in finding what the interesting patterns are, without the user thinking of the relevant questions first. In large databases, there are so many patterns that the user can never practically think of the right questions to ask. The four areas of decision support are as follows:

i. Automatic pattern discovery, whereby a program looks for patterns by itself with no queries posed by a user. This is an approach based on the System Initiative.

ii. Predictive Modeling, where predictions are made based on the analysis of previous data. In this case the system Initiative is used.

iii. Multidimensional analysis, whereby the program helps a user visualize patterns from various viewpoints. This is an example of a Mixed Initiative approach.

iv. Query and reporting, for providing answers to questions that would be posed by a user. This is a User Initiative approach.

A computer system that finds patterns in data is called a Discovery System. A computer system that aims to make predictions based on the patterns is called a Predictive Modeling System. These are two quite distinct forms of activities, and jointly form the Data Mining effort. The first approach may help a user change his/her perception with respect to the data, while the second may simply make a prediction. A hyper-information capability is very important in all systems. As a trend or a graph is displayed, the user has to be able to zoom in and get further information on demand. The data visualization system allows for interactive graphing of trends and patterns. The user can click on any segment of a graph to zoom in and get a further graph. The interface may be customized for the decision maker by end users and analysts. The data analysis system is used by the analysts to find significant trends and rules in the data being analyzed. The system complements statistical analysis by finding specific rules that categorize clusters of information.

A predictive modeling system may be an Algorithmic System developed by writing a specific program, e.g. a scoring model, in some programming language, or may be a Learning System trained by providing it with examples. In an

Algorithmic System human beings prepare the requisite models and the associated algorithms by the use of various techniques like performing statistical analysis. The algorithm is then coded into a program for execution. Later, new data is submitted for prediction. A Learning System, on the other hand, looks at historical data and is trained, or trains itself, to predict the future. At times, an underlying model needs to be supplied to the system, but there is no direct effort by humans for inventing and coding an algorithm. Learning Systems themselves can be categorized as:

i. **Opaque or Black box Systems**

   An Opaque System learns and predicts, but its specific behavior on each case is unknown to the user and it does not explain its behavior

ii. **Transparent or Explainable Systems**

   A Transparent System, on the other hand, can provide a detailed account of why it performs a specific operation and its internal methods of operation are visible to the user

It is essential to use a Transparent Discovery System with an explanation capability, as part of the Pre-Mining activity to be performed in steps 3 & 7 above. This will allow us to fully understand the data before warehousing it. In addition, predictive modeling should take place on the sample to confirm its suitability for the eventual analysis sessions. These two activities are the heart of the horizontal prototyping effort.

4.15 Data Mining - Architectural Considerations

In general, a data mining system may be viewed as a layer on top of the database query system. A query language such as SQL can deal with queries, but it cannot automatically form hypotheses since it does not know what to ask for. To discover information automatically the following steps are required:

i. Hypotheses Formation
ii. Query Generation & Statistics Generation

iii.   Result Generation and modification of hypothesis (if required).

iv.   Pattern generation(by repetition of the above processes)

The architecture of a discovery system should be fully scaleable in the sense that each of its modules should be able to take advantage of faster hardware. The architecture would comprise of three layers:

i. **User Interface**

The User Interface is used to interact with the user. It accepts information about the criteria to search for, the topics of interest, etc. and displays results to the user.

ii. **Discovery Module**

The Discovery Module constitutes the "brain" of the system. It makes decisions as to what patterns should be looked for and submits queries and statistical tests to the Search Engine. The interaction between the Discovery Module and the Search Engine is continuous and is based on the results obtained from the query being executed. The Discovery Module generates new queries and submits them to the Search Engine.

iii. **Search Engine**

The Search Engine is responsible for executing SQL queries and statistical questions within the database.

Since the architecture is fully scaleable all the three components may reside on a single system or the components may be fully distributed. This is essential for the development of prototypes wherein the development initiates with the three components on one computer before being distributed on to the final system. The Sandwich Paradigm advocates the development of a small architecture that can subsequently be scaled up.

4.16 Data Quality

The quality of the data in a warehouse affects the decision making capability of a mining system. It is therefore essential to employ data quality management methods during the prototyping phase. The data quality program must be an integral part of the data warehouse on an ongoing basis. Large databases are prone to several errors and inconsistencies which can be rectified through an intelligent database quality management system. Such a system comprises of three primary components as listed:

i.   Fundamental Quality Enforcement
ii.   Rule-based Constraints
iii. Automatic Error Detection

The fundamental quality system primarily checks for type consistency, range and validity while a rule-based constraint system applies known and user provided constraints. The automatic anomaly detection system aids in rule discovery and uncovers patterns based on these discoveries. Errors often manifest themselves as anomalies in the form of exceptions to expected patterns. Typographical errors are the most common in large databases. The anomalies in the data cause the rules to be rendered meaningless and hence anomaly detection is a useful form of data mining that supplements rule discovery. In practice, anomaly detection follows on from rule discovery. Once a set of rules has been extracted from a large database, the rules can then be applied to the same data (or to new data) to detect data anomalies.

It is general practice to choose one of the available methods, like Basic Quality Enforcement, Constraints or Automatic Error Detection for handling data errors based on 'gut feel'. However the best course of action to employ moderate measures of each component, followed by further analysis to determine the key areas of concern. Automatic Error Detection is important, since errors are usually where one does not expect them to be. It is thus essential to perform automatic anomaly detection when working with horizontal prototypes.

4.17 Summary

Over the years, many different approaches have been developed to extract meaningful information or knowledge from the massive data sets generated by organizations On-line Transaction Processing Systems. Initially, the primary source of access and analysis were simple report generators and query tools. The advent of Data Warehousing, the scope and breadth of their capabilities and potential impact on an organizations performance have increased tremendously over the last two decades. Multiple vendors have repackaged many existing tools as "business intelligence" or "knowledge management" tools to cater to this demand. Traditional queries are the simplest form of accessing a database to request information. Query and reporting tools enable users to formulate complex queries without having to interact with and create code using SQL programming language while offering formatting and presentation templates to display the results. Many packages offer the ability to port the results onto spreadsheets to take advantage of the graphical representation of the results, or have graphic capabilities included in them directly. This chapter explored the various strategies for data mining in conjunction with a data warehouse. The requirements, different data structures, computational processes that enable a data mining system to cater to differing group of users were also discussed

4.18 Exercise Questions

1. Explain the relation between data mining and data warehouse systems. How do they complement each other?
2. Briefly discuss the architecture of an Enterprise Decision Support System.
3. Discuss the differences between Exploratory and Confirmatory analyses.
4. What is meant by Sampling and Summarization?
5. Explain the importance of Data Quality.
6. What does the Sandwich Paradigm mean? Explain its relevance in the field of Data Mining?
7. Explain the concept behind Stand Alone Mining.

8. Illustrate the various methods of deploying a Data Mining system over a Data Warehouse.

Chapter Objectives

The objectives of this chapter are:

- *To understand the key Data Mining Functions including:*
  - *Data Preparation*
  - *Data Modeling*
  - *Data Selection*
  - *Data Cleansing*
  - *Results Visualization*
- *To describe the categorization of Data Mining including:*
  - *Analytical Tools*
    - *Decision Trees*
    - *Option Trees Neural Networks*
    - *Evidence (Naive-Bayes) Classifiers*
    - *Association Rules*
    - *Clustering*
    - *Data Manipulators*
  - *Visual Tools*
    - *Generic Visualization Tools*
    - *Dimensional Viewing*
    - *Multidimensional Scatter Plots*
    - *Map Visualizer*
    - *Tree Visualizer*
    - *Statistical Visualizers*
    - *Record Viewers*
- *To understand the essential characteristics of a visualizer:*
  - *3D Fly Thru*
  - *Drill Through*
  - *Animation Control*

Chapter 5

DATA MINING TOOLS

5.1 Introduction

Data mining software provides the means for transforming organizational data into tangible business information. Highly robust and stable commercial database platforms are now available for massively parallel processors including IBM DB2, INFORMIX-Online XPS, ORACLE RDBMS and SYBASE (SAP) Systems. This chapter provides a list of some of the most common tools used in the area of data mining along with a list of their key features. In the evolution from business data to business information, each new step has built upon the previous ones. Data mining tools provides automation of pattern detection within databases using defined approaches and algorithms. This provides a facility to explore current and historical data that can subsequently be analyzed to predict future trends. The ability of data mining tools to predict future trends and behaviors by parsing databases for hidden patterns provides organizations the ability to make proactive, knowledge-driven decisions while uncovering answer questions previously thought unanswerable.

5.2 Data Mining Functions

Data mining is an iterative process wherein the model and assumptions may be changed to highlight or uncover observations on the underlying data in relation to the results being viewed by the user. This interactive process is augmented by the deployment of a well designed integrated product suite to aid the data mining process. This required powerful analytical tools tightly integrated with excellent visualization tools encapsulated within an overall framework. This provides the user the freedom to focus on data analysis besides providing visibility to the data

135

mining process within the organization. The integration of visual aids forms an important consideration during the evaluation of potential tools for a business enterprise. The primary functions of a data mining tool are listed below:

i. **Data Preparation**

   Provide a visual overview of large volumes of data

ii. **Data Modeling**

   Provide a visual model of the source domain data set

iii. **Data Selection**

   Identify rough areas of interest in the data i.e. direct sampling of the original data set

iv. **Data Cleansing**

   Identify areas within the data population that require cleansing.

v. **Results Visualization**

   This involves the graphical display of the final results as desired by the end user

5.3 Categorization

Data Mining Tools can be categorized as follows:

i) **Analytical Tools**

   Data mining tools should have the functionality to build and apply several classification models, giving users the power to isolate goal-oriented patterns in large data sets. Following are some of the models used:

   a) *Decision Trees*

   Decision trees are models produced by a class of techniques such as regression trees (CART) and chi-squared automatic induction (CHAID). They are mostly used for directed data mining as in an attempt to classify data. An analyst selects an attribute to be the label. The values of that attribute determine the classes. The decision tree, by making intelligent splits on the data, attempts to isolate individual classes corresponding to the leaves of the tree.

b) Option Trees

Variations of decision trees are option trees. They emphasize the fact that several attributes may be reasonable, providing the users with a set of options and allowing them to decide which of the branches to pursue. Tree visualizers aid in the understanding of the presented data. Pointing to any object in the scene will show the probabilities, counts, and other information to be displayed allowing users to discover additional details about the overall accuracy of the model.

c) Neural Networks

Neural Networks are a very common form of data mining. They represent a computer based model of the interconnections of the human brain. These networks can be trained to recognize patterns for classification and prediction. Neural networks are capable of detecting patterns in the data in a manner similar to humans. Neural network is a highly active research discipline and hence subject to frequent advancements. One of the drawbacks is the difficulty an analyst has in understanding the models produced and thereby difficulty in trusting the results.

d) Evidence (Naive-Bayes) Classifiers

The Naive-Bayes induction algorithm provides a model that allows data classification based upon observed probabilities and supporting evidence for a particular classification. A visualizer can display the structure and properties built by an induction engine. The visualizers can display unique values or value ranges of attributes for particular classification through rows of 3D pie charts or bars representing the attributes used by the classifier. Interaction with the visual objects provides detailed information about the overall classification probabilities.

e) Association Rules

Most mining tools automatically analyze data, revealing product affinities and relationships between data entities. The most important task for developing association rules is determining which things go together. This is commonly referred to as "market basket analysis". The analogy is one of a shopping cart at a grocery store and determining what things go together. Stores can then use this affinity mapping to arrange items of the store's shelves. It also helps identify cross-selling opportunities that can potentially increase the revenue generated from each patron. Association rules are derived from the data, for example, sales of bread and butter occur frequently together. The discovery of such patterns can help generate association rules. A rule visualizer graphically displays results from the association rule generator. Analyzing rules discovered in the data mining process gives users greater insight into the nature of a particular data set. A rule visualizer quickly reveals the quantity and relative strengths of relationships between elements, helping users focus on important data entities and rules. The rules can be presented, for example, on a grid landscape, with left-hand side (LHS) items on one axis, and right-hand side (RHS) items on the other. Attributes of a rule can be displayed at the junction of its LHS and RHS item. Attributes are displayed using bars, disks, and labels. The 3-D rule grid can be zoomed, rotated, and panned. Visual filtering and querying allows for users to focus in on selected rules.

f) Clustering

Clustering is the process of segmenting a homogenous clusters data collection to form heterogeneous data sets. In clustering there is no pre-classification of data or distinction between variables; they are selected by their similarity to one another. Clustering is often used to prepare data for another step in analysis. In the credit card industry providers would want to divide the data set into clusters that match its products. For example, high net worth individuals, individuals owning luxury cars for offering its premium cards.

g) Data Manipulators

Some products are able to access data from the data warehouse directly, perform transformations such as binning and aggregation, and prepare the data for data mining and visualization. These products typically include interfaces with relational database software from most of the popular database platforms as well as flat files and files from other data mining applications.

ii) Visual Tools

Even with the advances in data mining, there are still human limitations to understanding and deciphering the rules and equations generated by the different tool sets. For that reason, visual tools have been developed to help detect and correct data anomalies in an efficient and quick fashion. This is similar to a spreadsheet that allows a user to visualize the results of the calculations via a pie chart or a bar graph as compared to viewing columns and rows of numbers. Visualization technology makes it easier to picture the relationships between data. For example, an organization might use data mining techniques to predict the sales of certain products from certain stores. The ability to do so accurately allows them to tune production and distribution capabilities to be able to supply their client stores with the entire product they need. This ensures optimal inventory levels and logistics. A three dimensional visualizer is used to highlight anomalies across multiple product and store categories and simplify the report formulation. Once the anomalous areas are highlighted, the analyst can focus their attention on the underlying causes for the anomaly/relationship. These tools can be classified as follows:

a) Generic Visualization Tools

Data sets are generally complex for representation in two or even three dimensions. Visualization technologies are ideal for simultaneously analyzing the behavior of data in multiple dimensions. Visual data mining tools depict the original data enabling users to interactively explore data and discover meaningful new patterns, trends, and relationships quickly. These tools utilize animated 3D landscapes that are optimized for human navigation to space, recognize patterns, track movements, and compare objects of different sizes and colors. Users have complete control over the data's appearance with visual tools

b) *Dimensional Viewing*

Dimensional viewing presents a graphical interface which displays data as a three-dimensional "landscapes" of arbitrarily specified and positioned "bar chart" shapes. This tool displays quantitative and relational characteristics of spatially oriented data. Data items are associated with graphical "bar chart" objects in the visual landscape with recognizable spatial shapes and positions, such as those found in geographical maps. The landscape consists of a collection of spatially related objects with individual customizations. The landscape can be navigated dynamically by:

- Drilling down to view minute details
- Drilling up to aggregate data into coarser-grained graphical objects
- Using animation to see how the data changes across many independent dimensions.

c) *Multidimensional Scatter Plots*

A scatter plot visualizer lets one visualize data by mapping each record, or row, in the dataset to an entity in the three-dimensional scatter plot. Variables in the data can be mapped to the sizes, colors, and the xyz coordinate positions of the entities. In the three-dimensional landscape, one can orient the display to emphasize particular dimensions or a point of view. A scatter plot tool helps in scaling the values of variables to enable better emphasis. It is desirable to be able to filter the display to show only those entities meeting certain criteria. Scatter visualizers can also serve as an invaluable tool for the discovery of dirty data, sometimes recognized as anomalies through unexplainable behavior.

d) *Map Visualizer*

With a map visualizer, users explore data having strong spatial relationships. Data is displayed as graphical elements on a visual map, with user-defined variables indicated by the height and color of each element. Users can drill down for more detailed graphical information about specific regions or drill up to see data in context.

Map visualizers facilitate greater insights into data with geographical significance. Multiple animations can be synchronized to present side-by-side trend comparisons. As an example, the data might contain information for sales of a product on a Pan India basis. However the geographies of each state, their demographic details are not included. The user supplies this information when the map is built. The data can then by mapped onto the map of India, providing a more intuitive view of the data.

e) *Tree Visualizer*

A Tree Visualizer displays hierarchical data structures in a 3D landscape, revealing quantitative and multi-dimensional characteristics of data. Utilizing a fly-through technique, users view data as visual representations of hierarchical nodes and associations. Users explore data with any level of detail or summary, from a bird's-eye perspective down to detailed displays of source data.

f) *Statistical Visualizers*

This class of visualizing technologies can be used to present basic statistical information about the data in a graphical format, including mean, median, standard deviations, histograms, and quartiles.

g) *Record Viewers*

At different stages in an analytical process, it becomes useful to examine the detail current set of data records. Throughout the transformation and visualization stages, users can refer to record viewers for a spreadsheet view of the underlying data sets.

An organization that initiates the data mining and visualization process will quickly realize the endless possibilities of advanced analysis. In these situations, it is important to have a toolset that can be integrated with other applications. Some products ship with Application Programming Interfaces (APIs) that allow developers to invoke data mining and data visualization functionality from within their proprietary base applications. The use of open architecture facilitates the co-existence of these products with other mining and visual tools. The essential characteristics of visualizer are as listed:

i) **3D Fly Thru**

This visualization feature presents data as clustered, hierarchical blocks (nodes) and bars through which one can dynamically navigate, viewing part, or all, of the data set. For example a tree visualizer displays quantitative and relational characteristics of data by showing them as hierarchically connected nodes in a tree structure. Each node contains bars whose height and color correspond to aggregations of data values. The lines connecting nodes show the relationship of one set of data to its subsets. Values in subgroups can be summed and displayed automatically in the next higher level. The base under the bars can provide information about the aggregate value of all the bars. Using a mouse, one can "fly" over and around the nodes, looking for the relationships that are of most interest to them. Focus on a particular set of bars in a node allows a user to drill through the bars to get the detailed granular data that comprises the aggregate. A tree visualizer takes data at the lowest level of the hierarchy as input. Data is then aggregated up through the visualization automatically, as specified by the user.

ii) Drill Through

Drill through is a method that facilitates users to complement and accelerate knowledge discovery by observing data patterns or node of interest. The users can subsequently expand "into" the specific data set. Data records at the source of an observed pattern are easily accessed using drill-through techniques, making data readily available for further transformation, analysis, and visualization.

iii) Animation Control

Animation provides users with the ability to discover trends, patterns, and anomalies in multiple dimensions. It allows users to discover data segmentations, clustering and information profiles. The animation of display across user-defined independent variables facilitates the observation of trends in extremely complex data sets. The current visualization technologies are capable of providing additional facilities for handling very large data sets. Snap-in tools facilitate the mapping of numeric variables onto sliders facilitating user access and administration. Animation control lets one-trace animation paths in multiple dimensions. A user can subsequently play back the path created and watch the size, color, and motion of the entities for isolating trends or anomalies.

5.4 Summary

The value of undiscovered relationships in corporate data warehouses is enormous. Most of the Fortune 500 Business enterprises generate business opportunities to the tune of millions of dollars annually through sound business decisions that is aided by decision support systems and mining tools. The powerful combination of database management systems, warehousing packages and data marts integrated with data mining technologies provided business significantly enhance the value of their decision processes. In earlier days simple visual tools were employed to identify patterns in the vast amounts of data within an organization. Integration of these visual packages with the powerful data mining and analytical tools have led to the development of newer packages that provide organizations with powerful analytical, knowledge discovery and decision making capabilities. Business enterprises can benefit from significantly enhanced financial performance by altering their product and service offerings in tune with customer requirements, while gaining the first mover advantage.

5.5   Exercise Questions

1. Briefly explain the categorization of Data Mining Tools.
2. Explain the key characteristics of Visual Mining Tools.
3. Write a small note on option trees.

This page is intentionally blank

References

1. Datawarehouse.com. (1995). *Warehousing & Mining*. Retrieved July 1998, from Datawarehouse.com: www.datawarehouse.com

2. Frawley, W. J., Piatetsky-Shapiro, G., & Matheus, C. J. (2001, Jan 31). *Artículo Introductorio sobre data Mining*. Retrieved May 25, 2009, from dc.uba.ar: http://www-2.dc.uba.ar/materias/dm/articulo.html

3. Kurt Thearling, Barry Becker, Dennis DeCoste, Bill Mawby, Michel Pilote, and Dan Sommerfield , *Proceedings of the Integration of Data Mining and Data Visualization Workshop*, Springer Verlag, 1998

4. Mac Lane, S. "*Categories for the Working Mathematician*, Springer, 1971.

5. Parsaye Kamran, DataMines for DataWarehouses , An Information Discovery, Inc. White Paper, Retrieved May 1998 from http://www.the-data-mine.com/Organizations/ InformationDiscoveryInc

6. Parsaye, K. "*Data Mines for Data Warehouses*", Database Programming & Design, September 1996.

7. Parsaye, K. "*Data Mines for Data Warehouses*", Database Programming & Design, September 1996

8. Parsaye, K. "*New Realms of Analysis*", Database Programming & Design, April 1996

9. Parsaye, K. "*The Sandwich Paradigm for Data Warehousing and Mining*", Database Programming and Design, April 1995

10. Parsaye, K. "*The Sandwich Paradigm*, Database Programming & Design, April 1995.

11. Parsaye, K. "*The Sandwich Paradigm*, Database Programming & Design, April 1995

12. Parsaye, K. et al. "*Intelligent Databases*, NY: John Wiley and Sons, 1989

13. Zentut. (n.d.). *Data Mining Processes*. Retrieved April 14, 2007, from Zentut: http://www.zentut.com/data-mining/data-mining-processes

Bibliography

1. Parsaye, K. *"New Realms of Analysis"*, Database Programming & Design, April 1996.

2. Mac Lane, S. *"Categories for the Working Mathematician*, Springer, 1971.

3. Parsaye, K. et al. *"Intelligent Databases*, NY: John Wiley and Sons, 1989.

4. Kurt Thearling, Barry Becker, Dennis DeCoste, Bill Mawby, Michel Pilote, and Dan Sommerfield

5. C. Brunk, J. Kelly, and R. Kohavi, "MineSet: An Integrated System for Data Access, Visual Data Mining, and Analytical Data Mining," Proceedings of the Third Conference on Knowledge Discovery and Data Mining (KDD-97), Newport Beach, CA, August 1997

6. D. DeCoste, "Mining multivariate time-series sensor data to discover behavior envelopes," Proceedings of the Third Conference on Knowledge Discovery and Data Mining (KDD-97), Newport Beach, CA, August 1997.

7. D. Rathjens, MineSet Users Guide, Silicon Graphics, Inc., 1997.

8. Parsaye, K., Chignell, M.H.: *"Intelligent Database Tools and Applications"*. New York: John Wiley and Sons, 1993 .

9. Parsaye, K. and Chignell, M.H. *"Data Quality with Smart Databases"*, Database Programming and Design, January 1995.

10. Parsaye, K. *"The Discovery Machine"*, Proceedings of AAAI Workshop on Knowledge Discovery, August 1989.

11. Parsaye, K., *"Large Scale Data Mining in Parallel"*, DBMS Magazine, February 1995.

12. Parsaye, K., Chignell, M.H. *"Concentric Design for Decision Support"*, Database Programming & Design, May 1993.

13. Parsaye, K. and Chignell, M.H. (1992). *"Information made Visual using HyperData"*. AI Expert, September, 1992.

14. Parsaye, K., Chignell, M.H., et al. (1989) *"Intelligent Databases: Object-Oriented, Deductive Hypermedia Technologies"*, New York, John Wiley & Sons 1989.

15. Parsaye, K.*"Surveying Decision Support: New Realms of Analysis"* Database Programming and Design, April 1996.

16. Parsaye, K. *"Large Scale Data Mining in Parallel"*, DBMS Magazine, March 1995.

Index